ITALIAN SOLDIER IN NORTH AFRICA 1941–43

P. CROCIANI AND P.P. BATTISTELLI ILLUSTRATED BY STEVE NOON

Series editor Marcus Cowper

First published in Great Britain in 2013 by Osprey Publishing,
PO Box 883, Oxford, OX1 9PL, UK
PO Box 3985, New York, NY 10185-3985, USA
Email: info@ospreypublishing.com

Osprey Publishing, part of Bloomsbury Publishing Plc

Transferred to digital print on demand 2015.

First published 2013
2nd impression 2014

Printed and bound by PrintOnDemand-Worldwide.com,
Peterborough, UK.

A CIP catalogue record for this book is available from the British
Library.

ISBN: 978 1 78096 855 1
E-book ISBN: 978 1 78096 857 5
PDF ISBN: 978 1 78096 856 8

Editorial by Ilios Publishing Ltd, Oxford, UK
(www.iliospublishing.com)
Index by Zoe Ross
Typeset in Myriad Pro and Sabon
Artwork by Steve Noon
Originated by PDQ Media, UK

Acknowledgements

The authors wish to acknowledge Lieutenant-Colonel
Filippo Cappellano, head of the archive of the army
historical branch (Archivio dell'Ufficio Storico dello
Stato Maggiore Esercito) for his valuable contribution
and support.

The Woodland Trust

Osprey Publishing is supporting the Woodland Trust,
the UK's leading woodland conservation charity, by
funding the dedication of trees.

www.ospreypublishing.com

Artist's note

Readers may care to note that the original paintings from which the
colour plates in this book were prepared are available for private
sale. The Publishers retain all reproduction copyright whatsoever. All
enquiries should be addressed to:

Steve Noon, www. steve-noon.co.uk

The Publishers regret that they can enter into no correspondence
upon this matter.

Authors' note

In Italian, to form the plural of male nouns (which generally end in O
or E) the last letter usually changes to an I (i.e. divisione, divisioni);
in female nouns (which usually end in A) the last letter changes to an
E (i.e. compagnia, compagnie). Nouns like Bersaglieri and Arditi are
plural. The basic army commands and units include an army
(armata), an army corps (corpo d'armata), a division (divisione), a
regiment (reggimento) and its equivalent group (gruppo or
raggruppamento), a battalion (battaglione), a company (compagnia),
a platoon (plotone), and squad (squadra). Cardinal numbers have an
° (male nouns) or an ª (female nouns) after the number.

In the text names have been translated for clarity (like: armata =
army, corpo d'armata = army corps, divisione = division), the only
abbreviation commonly used being Superasi (Comando Superiore
Forze Armate Africa Settentrionale Italiana), which was the Italian
Commander-in-Chief in North Africa until 16 August 1942 when,
following the invasion of Egypt, it became C-in-C Libya while an
Italian liaison HQ was established linking the Panzer Armee Afrika
directly to the Italian chief of general staff (Delease, Delegazione
del Comando Supremo in Africa Settentrionale).

Readers are suggested to check these other Osprey titles: Piero
Crociani, Pier Paolo Battistelli, Warrior 144 *Italian Blackshirt 1935–45*;
Philip Jowett, Men-at-Arms 353 *The Italian Army 1940–45 (3) Italy
1943–45*; Piero Crociani, Pier Paolo Battistelli, Elite 99 *Italian Army
Elite Units and Special Forces 1940–43*.

Rank comparison chart (approximate)		
Italian Army (carabinieri)	British Army	US Army
Soldato	Private	Private
Soldato scelto	Lance Corporal	Private 1st Class
Caporale (carabiniere)	Corporal	Corporal
Caporalmaggiore (appuntato)	Lance Sergeant	Sergeant
Sergente (vice brigadiere)	Sergeant	Technical Sergeant
Sergente maggiore (brigadiere)	Staff Sergeant	Master Sergeant
Maresciallo	Warrant Officer III *	
Maresciallo capo grade	Warrant Officer II	Warrant Officer junior
Maresciallo maggiore	Warrant Officer I	Chief Warrant Officer
Sottotenente	Second Lieutenant	Second Lieutenant
Tenente	Lieutenant	First Lieutenant
Capitano	Captain	Captain
Maggiore	Major	Major
Tenente colonnello	Lieutenant-Colonel	Lieutenant-Colonel
Colonnello	Colonel	Colonel
Generale di brigata	Brigadier	Brigadier-General
Generale di divisione	Major-General	Major-General
Generale di corpo d'armata	Lieutenant-General	Lieutenant-General
Generale d'armata	General	General
Maresciallo d'Italia	Field Marshal	General of the Army
* until 1941		

CONTENTS

ITALIAN SOLDIER IN NORTH AFRICA 1941–43

INTRODUCTION

It is undeniable that the image of the Italian soldier – not just in North Africa – is and will always be tainted by the spectacular success achieved by Major-General Richard O'Connor's Western Desert Force between December 1940 and February 1941. With a brilliant campaign that can be compared only with the German drive across the Ardennes and the dash to the Channel in May 1940, O'Connor managed to destroy an entire Italian army driving across Cyrenaica, and to threaten Tripoli itself. Without detracting from this success in any way it should be noted that, as with the French Army, Graziani's army in North Africa suffered from outdated doctrines and tactics which shifted the balance in Western Desert Force's favour, probably the only unit actually equal to the German Panzer divisions at the time.

However, what followed is also relevant; judging from the many histories and accounts of the war in North Africa, following the arrival in Libya of the German Afrika Korps and Erwin Rommel in February 1941, the presence of the Italians on the battlefield, seems to be incidental, if it exists at all. It is not uncommon for them to be regarded as a kind of irritation, or even impediment, to those who were really fighting the war – the Germans and the British. Such attitudes can be explained in several ways, not least by the failure of the Italians to develop a real military history of their own, comparable to that of the British and the Germans. Needless to say such a point of view is completely incorrect, for the very simple reason that the Italian soldier did play a part in the war in North Africa, even after the arrival of the Afrika Korps.

It would be wrong to claim that Rommel's Afrika Korps did not play a decisive role in the war in the Western Desert, but it would also be wrong to underestimate the part the Italians played in North Africa in 1941–43. For example, while Western Desert Force's fighting power was reduced after the formation of Eighth Army, the fighting power of the Italian army in North Africa would increase. Without going into detail, it is true that such an increase was limited, mostly by a series of shortcomings that were deeply rooted in the Italian army, the most fundamental being the slow rate of transformation from a colonial army to one capable of fighting a mechanized war.

Conquered during the Italian–Turkish war of 1911–12, Libya became an Italian colony mostly on paper for it was not until 1923, a year after

A *sergente maggiore* of the motor transport corps being decorated with the Iron Cross by a German officer. He is wearing the continental grey-green uniform with a cross-chest ammunition pouch, and the pistol holster attached to the end. (Filippo Cappellano)

Mussolini's rise to power, that the Italian army started a systematic seizure of the entire country, countering a local rebellion which was eventually overcome in 1932. Two years later the newly appointed governor general and military commander in Libya, Air Marshal Italo Balbo, started a massive colonization with thousands of Italians moving there. The military organization of the country was the final stage; regular army units were sent to Libya only when needed, any other operation being undertaken by the Regio Corpo Truppe Libiche, the locally raised Libyan forces subordinated to the colonial ministry. Only in 1937–39 would Balbo, along with the chief of army staff, develop a strategic plan aimed at seizing the Suez Canal, a plan eventually thwarted by the comment by the Italian navy that, in the event of war, facing the threat of both the French navy and the Mediterranean Fleet, it would not be possible to supply Libya. The fall of France altered the strategic balance, but it was already too late to make good the many shortcomings afflicting the Italian army.

A long-serving veteran *sergente maggiore* attached to the Giovani Fascisti regiment in 1942; he is armed with the new 9mm Beretta 39 MP, and is wearing a *camiciotto sahariano* along with the black fez typical of the regiment. (Filippo Cappellano)

CHRONOLOGY

1940

10 June	Italy declares war on France and Great Britain.
28 June	Air Marshal Italo Balbo, Italian commander in Libya, is killed. Maresciallo d'Italia Rodolfo Graziani replaces him.
13–16 September	Italian advance into Egypt, to Sidi Barrani.
9 December	Start of Operation *Compass*; the Western Desert Force attacks Sidi Barrani.

1941

3–5 January	Seizure of Bardia by the 6th Australian Division.
22 January	Seizure of Tobruk.
25 January	Major-General O'Connor, the British commander, drives across the desert to Beda Fomm; the remnants of the Italian Tenth Army withdraws west.
6 February	Seizure of Benghazi.
7 February	The remnants of Tenth Army are destroyed at Beda Fomm.
11 February	Arrival of the Afrika Korps, Generale Italo Gariboldi replaces Graziani as C-in-C Libya.
1 March	Free French forces seize the oasis of Kufra, in the Fezzan.
2 April	Rommel's drive into Cyrenaica.
10 April	Tobruk besieged, Axis troops reach the Libyan–Egyptian border.
30 April	Axis attack against Tobruk fortress, battle of Ras El Mdauuar.
15–17 May	British attack against Sollum, Operation *Brevity*.
15–17 June	Operation *Battleaxe*, second British attack against Sollum.
27 July	Generale Ettore Bastico replaces Generale Gariboldi as C-in-C Libya.

15 August	The Panzer Gruppe Afrika is formed, along with the Italian Corpo d'Armata di Manovra (CAM).
18 November	Start of Operation *Crusader*, Eighth Army offensive to relieve Tobruk.
19 November	First tank clash between Italian and British troops at Bir El Gubi.
7 December	Rommel orders withdrawal back to El Agheila, Japan attacks the United States.
28–30 December	Axis troops halt Eighth Army's advance at Mersa Brega, Italian XXI Corpo deployed at the front.

1942

2–17 January	Axis troops at Bardia and Sollum surrender, the Italian 'Savona' division is destroyed.
21 January	Rommel's second drive in Cyrenaica; Italian CAM is redesignated XX Corpo.
31 January	Panzer Gruppe Afrika is redesignated Panzer Armee Afrika.
6 February	Axis advance halts at the Gazala Line.
27 May	Start of the Axis attack against the Gazala Line.
20–21 June	Tobruk seized by Axis troops, Rommel advances into Egypt.
25–28 June	Mersa Matruh is seized by the Axis forces.
1–31 July	First battle of El Alamein, the Axis advance is checked, and following Eighth Army's counterattacks the Axis forces face a serious crisis.
31 August to 4 September	Battle of Alam Halfa.
1 October	Panzer Armee Afrika is redesignated German-Italian Panzer Armee (Armata Corazzata Italo-Tedesca, ACIT).
23 October	Start of Operation *Lightfoot*, the second battle of El Alamein.
2–4 November	Start of Operation *Supercharge*; remnants of the Axis forces withdraw from El Alamein.
8 November	Allied landings in Morocco and Algeria.
11–12 November	Tunis bridgehead is formed.

1943

23 January	Tripoli evacuated by Axis forces.
4–5 February	Axis redeployment on the Mareth Line, the German-Italian Panzer Armee is reorganized as First Italian Army.
15 February	German counterattack in Tunisia.
20–27 March	Battle of the Mareth Line, Axis forces withdraw.
5–6 April	Battle of the Wadi Akarit, Axis forces retreat to the Enfidaville Line.
19 April	Eighth Army attacks the Enfidaville Line while Allied forces launch the final offensive against the Tunis bridgehead.
13 May	Surrender of the Axis forces in Tunisia.

THE ITALIAN ARMY IN NORTH AFRICA

The first sizeable Italian army units stationed in Libya were deployed in 1937, and included two army corps (XX and XXI) with four infantry divisions: 60ª 'Sabratha', 61ª 'Sirte', 62ª 'Marmarica', 63ª 'Cirene'. Not until spring 1939 were four other army divisions added (17ª 'Pavia', 25ª 'Bologna', 27ª 'Brescia', 55ª 'Savona') in the wake of mobilization, along with three other corps (X, XXII and XXIII) and two army commands, Fifth and Tenth. Furthermore, four Blackshirt divisions were formed using Fascist militia and army personnel, as well as two formed from Libyan soldiers. Between 1 September 1939 and 10 June 1940, the day Italy declared war on France and Great Britain, more than 250,000 men were sent to Libya along with 1,183 motor vehicles, 120 tanks and almost 800 guns, mostly in the first few days of June. This strength was not matched by actual fighting power; in May 1940 one of the Blackshirt divisions was disbanded, its personnel used to replenish the remaining three and to form the cadre of another army division, the 64ª 'Catanzaro', still incomplete in the summer of 1940. On 10 June 1940 there were 165,000 army soldiers plus 11,000 recruits in Libya, along with 16,000 Blackshirts and 24,000 Libyans.

Early developments would eventually be fateful; on 28 June 1940 Italo Balbo was killed and replaced by Maresciallo d'Italia Rodolfo Graziani, an expert in colonial warfare who had fought in Libya and Ethiopia in the 1930s. Graziani modelled the offensive into Egypt on Kitchener's advance in Sudan, aggravating the already sluggish, 'lead from the rear' Italian command system. Lack of motor transport eventually led to a colonial-warfare-style offensive; in summer 1940 there were only 7,000 lorries available in Libya (3,000 were light), and the Italian divisions were organized as 'divisioni autotrasportabili AS (Africa Settentrionale)', infantry divisions lacking motor transport of their own but suited to motorization using a motor transport pool. For this reason Graziani did not shift the bulk of the newly formed, and better trained, divisions against Egypt, rather stripping them of most of their assets. Also, he had the less highly trained and less suitable divisions (Blackshirts and Libyans) joining the first wave ('Marmarica' and 'Cirene') in the short-lived offensive that halted at Sidi Barrani. Reinforcements were sent from Italy, including (from June to December 1940) some 25,000 troops, 2,800 lorries, 163 tanks (mostly medium), 230 anti-tank and 470 guns. Actual strength decreased, with many from the senior levies discharged from duty.

Army strength in August 1940 was 167,000 (total armed forces 181,500 plus 24,500 Libyans), rising to 193,000 in September (total 211,000 plus 34,000 Libyans) but decreasing in October to 188,000, plus 27,000 Libyans, while in November the Brigata Corazzata Speciale (special tank brigade) was formed. On 9 December 1940, when Operation *Compass* began, Tenth Army had two Libyan and one Blackshirt division at Sidi Barrani; right behind were the 'Catanzaro' and 'Cirene' infantry divisions and, on the

Watching the battle unfold from high ground, Egypt 1942. In the foreground, watching through binoculars, is an unidentified general; his officers wear a combination of grey-green and khaki tropical uniforms. (Filippo Cappellano)

A *Bersaglieri* heavy machine-gun team firing an 8mm Fiat-Revelli model 35; belt fed and with a maximum fire rate of 450 rounds per minute, it was extremely prone to overheating. Note the grey-green uniforms. (Filippo Cappellano)

border, the 'Marmarica' and two Blackshirt divisions (farther west, at Gambut and Derna, were the 'Sirte' and 'Sabratha' divisions). Taking advantage of the fragmentation of the Italian units, and of their sluggish reaction and inept command, the Western Desert Force was able to destroy the enemy forces piecemeal and eventually to cut the retreat to the remnants of Tenth Army at Beda Fomm on 7 February 1941. Italian losses stood at some 110,000 to 130,000 men, almost 400 tanks and 900 guns; the two Libyan, three Blackshirt and 'Sirte', 'Marmarica', 'Cirene' and 'Catanzaro' divisions had been destroyed, leaving only remnants of the 'Sabratha'.

Reinforcements and replacements were sent from Italy, while in February the first units of the German Afrika Korps also arrived. At the end of February the Italian army in Libya was 105,000 strong (total 113,000 plus 16,000 Libyans), 24,000 of whom fought mostly with the newly arrived 132^a Divisione Corazzata 'Ariete' and Divisione di Fanteria 'Brescia', both only partly combat effective. Both would take part in Rommel's drive to Cyrenaica that led to the encirclement of Tobruk and to reaching the Libyan–Egyptian border, also taking part in the first, unsuccessful attempts to seize the Australian-held fortress along with the 102^a Divisione Fanteria Motorizzata 'Trento', newly arrived in mid-April. Because of the stalemate, other Italian units were brought forward and, in June, the deployment was as follows: the 'Savona' west of El Agheila, X Corpo and 'Bologna' division at Barce, the 'Pavia' at Derna, the 'Ariete', 'Brescia', 'Pavia' and 'Trento' divisions encircling Tobruk. By the end of June 1941 another 47,000 men had been sent to Libya along with 1,500 machine guns, 90 mortars, 375 anti-tank guns, 493 other guns, 5,000 lorries and 387 AFVs. By mid-June total Italian strength in Libya was 136,500; armament included 7,000 light and heavy machine guns, 780 mortars, 280 tanks (100 of which were medium), two armoured cars, 1,848 guns (including 436 anti-tank and 556 anti-aircraft guns) and 8,600 lorries, 3,330 of which were not in working order. However, only 61,500 men (45 per cent) were at the front; another 19,000 were garrisoned in Tripoli and the Sahara (14 per cent), and 20,000 others (14.5 per cent) were with the territorial army, the navy and air force. Logistical support was 36,000 strong, or 26.5 per cent.

The average strength of the infantry divisions was 6,000 ('Savona' bottom with 5,986, 'Bologna' top with 6,814), about 5,000 short of their established strength. Both the 'Trento' (8,824 out of 10,500) and the 'Ariete' (5,794 out of 7,439) were in similar shape. The latter also suffered heavy losses, had virtually no motor vehicles and would subsequently become an infantry division. In August the 101^a Divisione Fanteria Motorizzata 'Trieste' also arrived in Libya, while on 15 August, when Panzer Gruppe Afrika was formed, the Corpo d'Armata di Manovra (CAM, 'manoeuvre army corps', from 10 March 1942 XX Corpo d'Armata) was also formed with the motorized 'Trieste' and armoured 'Ariete' divisions under command. Deployed around Tobruk was XXI Corpo d'Armata (army corps) with the 'Pavia', 'Bologna', 'Brescia' and 'Trento' divisions, while the 'Savona' was deployed at Sollum. On 15 November 1941 Italian army strength was 132,410 (total 150,000 plus 16,000 Libyans), with a slightly different breakdown; under direct command of Superasi (the Comando Superiore Africa Settentrionale, Commander-in-Chief North Africa) the logistic and support units were some 27,000 (20.5 per cent) strong, plus the Tripoli defence troops (31,000 strong or 23.5 per cent, including the cadre of 'Sabratha' division), the Sahara troops 1,100 strong (1 per cent, plus the bulk of Libyan troops), and the Cyrenaica rear troops 7,300 strong (5 per cent).

The CAM, XXI Corpo and 'Savona' division were 66,000 strong, or 50 per cent of the total strength. The CAM was 23,951 strong, with the 'Ariete' at 6,231 and the still-untested 'Trieste' stood at 10,809. The first of these had 63 light tanks and 141 medium, 173 anti-tank 47/32 and 29 field guns, and 633 serviceable and 317 non-serviceable motor vehicles (cars and lorries). The 'Trieste' had 48 x 47/32 anti-tank and 42 field guns, 1,141 serviceable and 50 non-serviceable motor vehicles, while the 'Trento' was 9,040 strong, had 25 light tanks, 68 x 47/32 anti-tank and 36 field guns, 394 serviceable and 890 non-serviceable motor vehicles. The 'Bologna' was 6,546, the 'Pavia' 6,383, and the 'Brescia' 6,585 strong; the first had 392 machine guns and 82 mortars, while the 'Pavia' had only 255 machine guns and 75 mortars, and the 'Brescia' 366 machine guns and 121 mortars. Artillery was uneven too; the 'Bologna' had 49 anti-tank, 6 infantry and 37 field guns, both the 'Pavia' and 'Brescia' having 26 anti-tank and 8 infantry guns each, the former with 40 and the latter with 24 field guns. The 'Savona' had 6,334 men at Sollum and 2,520 at Bardia; armament included 332 machine guns, 84 mortars, 15 light tanks, 11 anti-tank, 22 infantry, and 37 field guns.

Not surprisingly, following the start of Eighth Army's *Crusader* offensive on 18 November 1941, the British and Commonwealth units tended to underestimate their Italian counterparts, while overestimating the Germans; however, in spite of heavy casualties, this time even the footslogged infantry divisions made their way back to El Agheila, apart from the 'Savona' trapped at Sollum and eventually surrendering in January 1942. By 28 December 1941

A group of motorcycle-mounted *Bersaglieri* in North Africa, 1941. The fast-moving Bersaglieri used both motorcycles and lorries for motor transport, but also bicycles. Many are wearing grey-green uniform jackets with khaki tropical trousers. (Ernesto G. Vitetti)

A *Bersaglieri* strongpoint in Tunisia; the *Bersaglieri* at the centre is manning a captured Boys Mk I anti-tank rifle and, on both sides, two others are armed with a 9mm Beretta 38 MP. The man in the foreground wears a windbreaker jacket over his tropical uniform. (Filippo Cappellano)

overall Italian combat strength dropped from 57,800 to 24,000, with some divisions down to a few men; 'Brescia' had 3,810, 'Bologna' 1,820, 'Pavia' 3,400, 'Trento' 4,220, 'Trieste' 2,200, 'Ariete' 1,500 (with 3 medium tanks in running order), and corps troops dropped from 12,195 to 7,000. Overall losses for the *Crusader* battles were 1,200 killed, 2,700 wounded and 19,800 missing ('Savona' included); thus far Italian army losses in North Africa were estimated at 2,748 killed (plus 915 in January 1942), 3,597 wounded (plus 1,760), and 124,362 missing (plus 9,272).

Reinforcements could not make good the losses, with 9,500 men out of 39,000 lost at sea from July to December 1941. Weapon and equipment losses were high too: 300 out of 2,862 lorries and 40 out of 129 tanks, with most of the 489 anti-tank guns and 236 field and anti-aircraft guns reaching Tripoli. By mid-January 1942 Italian army strength in Libya was 110,000; XX, XXI and the newly arrived X Corpo were 36,000 strong, divisions being down to an average strength of 3,000–5,000; only 93 medium tanks, 290 anti-tank and 190 field guns, 836 serviceable and 455 non-serviceable motor vehicles were available. Lack of personnel suggested an overall reorganization, with the divisions reducing established strength while increasing firepower. The new 'Divisione fanteria tipo AS 42' (North Africa model 42 infantry division) had an established strength of 6,942; armament

A ### CAPORALE MITRAGLIERE, 'BOLOGNA' DIVISION, 1940

This corporal machine-gunner wears the standard (until late 1941) tropical uniform of the Italian army, modelled after the European grey-green uniform; this consisted of a jacket, open at the neck, with four pleated pockets (with flaps) made of greenish-khaki cotton and worn over a cotton shirt, along with greenish-khaki cotton breeches and standard grey-green puttees with brown boots. In wintertime a grey-green uniform was widely used as well, often along with a greenish-khaki overcoat. The tropical pith helmet, worn with the national cockade and metal badge of the corps (1), was a much-appreciated item amongst Italian soldiers. The lapel badges showed a specific unit, corps or a specific branch; infantry divisions had their own colours (2), which were worn by both infantry regiments or, for other corps or branches, with their specific badge superimposed. These are the badges of the 'Bologna' division. The 6.5mm Breda 30 light machine gun was the standard platoon support weapon, with two assigned to each one of the two rifle squads making up the platoon. Roughly the equivalent of the Bren gun, although not as effective, it had a rate of 400–500 rounds per minute but was greatly hampered by complicated reloading; instead of a magazine the weapon used ammunition clips put into ammunition boxes from a cardboard container (4), clips were then inserted into the folding magazine (5) that had to be swung forward, loaded using the clip and then swung back into firing position. This complicated procedure was, along with the need constantly to lubricate the weapon through an enclosed oil box (causing all sorts of difficulty in the desert, in particular jamming), the main weakness of the weapon, requiring the two machine guns in a squad to be fired alternately. Leather gloves with a metal mail (3), carried in a special pouch worn on the belt, were needed to replace the barrels (7) approximately every 1,000 rounds. The machine-gun team was made up of three men including, apart from a machine-gunner (carrying only one Beretta 34 pistol in a holster), a leader carrying an ammunition box, and a loader carrying spare parts and a box containing two extra barrels, both armed with rifles. Carrying hand grenades, like the Breda 35 and the SRCM 35 (6), usually in a bread bag, added extra firepower when needed.

A 47/32 anti-tank gun position in the desert, showing the typical arrangement for this gun: a semicircular trench protected by sandbags and a raised position at the centre, which made it possible to turn the gun swiftly by 180 degrees. (Filippo Cappellano)

included 238 machine guns, 72 anti-tank rifles, 18 heavy mortars, 72 anti-tank and 60 field guns, plus 359 motor vehicles. The new motorized division 'AS 42' (the 'Trieste') was 6,671 strong, with 136 machine guns, 36 anti-tank rifles, 18 heavy mortars, 36 anti-tank and 60 field guns, 52 medium tanks, 47 armoured cars and 828 motor vehicles. 'Ariete's' strength was 8,289, with 80 machine guns, 18 anti-tank rifles, 42 anti-tank and 40 field guns, 20 heavy and 19 light self-propelled guns, 189 medium tanks and 47 armoured cars.

Overall reorganization also included bringing the depleted 'Sabratha' up to strength to replace the lost 'Savona' division, while new units were to arrive from Italy; the 133ª 'Littorio' armoured division, one-third of which was in Libya by April 1942, and the 16ª Divisione Fanteria Motorizzata 'Pistoia'. At the end of April 1942 reorganization was already well under way both for the 'Ariete' and the 'Trieste', at 80 per cent of their strength plus 70–80 per cent of their vehicles and guns ('Ariete's' armour units had been replenished by those of 'Littorio'), while infantry divisions were well behind schedule. 'Bologna' and 'Sabratha' had only 55 per cent of their strength, about half their guns and 20–25 per cent of their vehicles, while 'Brescia', 'Pavia' and 'Trento' had 60–65 per cent of their strength, 80 per cent ('Brescia') or 60–65 per cent of their guns, and 40–45 per cent of their motor vehicles. The problem was, once again, shortages of reinforcements and supplies from Italy; in 1942 troops mostly arrived by air, thus reaching the required 50,000 men, but vehicles and supplies fell short of plans; between January and April 1942 only 6,000 vehicles out of the 11,000 planned, and only 248,000 tons of supplies out of 360,000 had reached Libya. Italian units should have completed reorganization by autumn 1942, but Rommel's attack against the Gazala line came early on 27 May.

On 1 June 1942 the Italian army in Libya was 140,000 strong (plus some 14,000 Libyans), with the combat forces of X, XXI and XX Corpo d'Armata totalling some 44,500 men (32 per cent). Held in reserve were the 'Bologna' and the still-forming 136ª Divisione Giovani Fascisti (Young Fascists), both together 6,564 strong, plus elements of the 'Littorio' armoured division at Tripoli (4,125 men, together 8 per cent). The rest was made up of the logistical support (44,000 strong, 31 per cent), Tripoli defence command (25,000 strong, 18 per cent), Sahara (4,400 strong, 3 per cent) and Cyrenaica defences (11,300 strong, 8 per cent). Apart from the shrinking of the combat army component, available reserves suggest how severely lack of motorization influenced Italian fighting power. Six days into the Gazala battle most Italian units were well below established strength; 'Brescia' and 'Pavia' divisions had 4,700 and 4,400 men, 39 and 36 anti-tank guns and a total of 77 other guns. The 'Sabratha' was only 3,500 strong, with 35 anti-tank and 18 field guns, while the 'Trento' was 5,000 strong, with 64 anti-tank and 44 field guns. The 'Bologna', held in reserve, was 4,500 strong and had 60 anti-tank and 63 field guns, while the Giovani Fascisti had 30 anti-tank and 54 field guns. The 'Trieste', with 6,700 men, was almost at full strength with 29 tanks, 31 armoured cars, 88 anti-tank and 55 field guns, while the 'Ariete' was only 6,600 strong, having 137 tanks, 36 armoured cars, 237 anti-tank and 45 field guns. Of the initial 228, 62 tanks had already been lost, rising to 164 after the seizure of Tobruk. By then the 'Ariete' had only 50 tanks, 10 self-propelled guns, 17 armoured cars, 19 anti-tank and 33 guns left, while the 'Trieste' had 19 tanks, 11 armoured cars, 33 anti-tank and 42 field guns.

Infantry soldiers loading a truck with food supplies, apparently Parmesan cheese. All are wearing the 1940 greenish-khaki tropical uniform with tropical pith helmets and grey-green puttees. (Filippo Cappellano)

A field kitchen at work in the desert, with two Weiss field bakeries in background. They were not motorized, which meant they met with consistent delays reaching the advancing troops. They also used either wood or coal as fuel, neither of which was available in the desert. (Filippo Cappellano)

On 1 July Rommel's Panzer Armee Afrika arrived at El Alamein, finding stiffened resistance and facing its first real crisis; on the 10th the Australian attack against Tel El Eisa hit in particular the depleted 'Sabratha' division, almost destroying it. On 17 July the 'Brescia' division was left with one infantry battalion, the 'Pavia' with two, the 'Trento' was relatively intact, while the 'Sabratha' was disbanded on 25 July. The 'Ariete' had one infantry and one artillery battalion plus 15 tanks, the 'Trieste' three infantry and one artillery battalion, and the newly deployed (still incomplete) 'Littorio' division had one infantry battalion and 20 tanks. In the face of the crisis, the Italian reaction was to bring the 'Bologna' division forward while rushing in the 185ª Divisione Paracadutisti 'Folgore' from Italy by air as well as stripping the still-arriving 16ª Divisione Fanteria Motorizzata 'Pistoia' of its assets.

Actual combat strength was maintained, with 43,000 men in Egypt (32 per cent) out of the 136,000 (plus 13,000 Libyans) available to the Italian army in North Africa by 1 August 1942. Logistic and rear-area commands were 40,000 strong, with the Giovani Fascisti and 'Pistoia' divisions (2,200 and 8,600 strong) in reserve. Cyrenaica command was 14,600 strong, with the Tripoli and Sahara defences amounting to 27,600 altogether. Of the divisions, only the 'Trento' and 'Bologna' were in good shape being 5,200 and 4,700 strong, while the 'Brescia' was 4,300, and the 'Pavia' less than 3,000 strong. The 'Ariete' was at full strength with almost 7,200 men, but had only 56 tanks and 11 armoured cars, the 'Littorio' had 4,600 men, 71 light and 104 medium tanks. The 'Trieste' was 5,300 strong, had 6 tanks and 16 armoured cars. By then, 1,300 men of the 'Folgore' division had reached Alamein. After the battle of Alam Halfa the Giovani Fascisti division (on paper only) was sent to Siwa oasis, while the depleted 'Pistoia' was deployed behind the front and two more divisions arrived: the 80ª 'La Spezia' airlanding infantry (intended for use against Malta), and the 131ª Corazzata 'Centauro', both at Tripoli by 23 October.

The Italian army in North Africa was kept up to strength mostly by reinforcements; from May to November 1942 less than 40,000 men were sent, along with 933 anti-tank and 632 other guns, 1,040 tanks and 3,903 lorries. When the second battle of El Alamein started, the army's overall strength was 128,000; 99,000 men were in Egypt, 46,000 of whom were at the front (36 per cent overall strength, 46 local). X Corpo, deployed in the south with the 'Brescia' and 'Folgore' divisions (plus the 'Pavia' in the rearguard), was 16,000 strong, XXI ('Trento' and 'Bologna') in the north, 13,600 strong. Mobile XX Corpo (total strength 18,500, 'Trieste' division was deployed along the coast) had the 'Ariete', 7,200 strong, and the 'Littorio' with less than 4,500; both had some 14 light and 255 medium tanks, and 33 self-propelled guns. At the end of the Alamein battle almost all these divisions had been destroyed, leaving the 'Trieste', 'Pistoia' and Giovani Fascisti to withdraw to Libya to join 'La Spezia' and 'Centauro'. By mid-December 1942

overall strength was down to less than 99,000, including some 33,000 with the reorganized XX and XXI Corpi, plus 7,000 replacements, the 19,000 men of Tripoli and Sahara defences, and 37,000 in the rear. Meanwhile, following the German creation of the Tunis bridgehead, the 1ª Divisione di Fanteria 'Superga' arrived in Tunisia spearheading XXX Corpo, also including the LI infantry brigade; in December 1942 16,000 Italians landed in Tunisia, followed by 12,000 more in January 1943. On 5 February 1943, shortly after withdrawal from Libya, the Panzer Armee Afrika was reorganized into the First Italian Army (XXX Corpo was put under command of the German 5. Panzer Armee); its strength was 90,000, with both the XX ('Trieste' and Giovani Fascisti divisions) and XXI Corpo ('Pistoia' and 'La Spezia') totalling 33,000, the 'Centauro' (7,400 strong) being broken up to support other divisions and being eventually disbanded on 18 April. Early in March 1943 First Army maintained its strength, but mid-April estimates saw it shrinking to 70,000, plus some additional 35,800 Italian troops in the bridgehead. Less than a month later the Axis forces in Tunisia surrendered.

From 10 June 1940 to 13 May 1943 a grand total of 252,839 men were sent to North Africa, along with (amongst others) 9,314 machine guns, 1,530 mortars, 2,322 anti-tank and 1,694 other guns, 16,494 lorries and 1,960 tanks.

A 6.5mm Breda 30 light machine-gun position in the desert, showing the typical arrangement of a shallow hole dug in the sand protected by stones. On the left an officer wearing a *sahariana* jacket with a side cap; the soldiers seem to be in their shirtsleeves. (Filippo Cappellano)

RECRUITMENT, ENLISTMENT AND CONDITIONS OF SERVICE

The Italian Army was an army of draftees, with a cadre of career officers and non-commissioned officers. With preliminary selection at the age of 18, at 20 draftees were called to arms for one year of service under the colours; at this stage they were assigned to a regiment, usually composed of draftees from three or more different areas of the country. Draftees could be recalled to duty whenever necessary, mostly as a result of mobilization. There were two groups of officers: career officers, mostly from the academies, and substantive (or complementary) officers. Substantive officers were selected from people with higher education, serving under the colours as second lieutenants after a seven-month course. By choice, and after selection, some could join the colours permanently. Most of the NCOs were drafted from the rank and file, particularly those promoted after the wars in Ethiopia and Spain, serving either as sergeants or warrant officers (*marescialli*). A limited number of rank and file (mostly specialists) could re-enlist for another one, two or three years.

Draftees recalled to duty in the first mobilization in 1939–40 were mainly aged 21 to 30, with a small intake aged 31 to 45. In September 1940, after the class of 1920 had been called to duty, the army had a surplus of more than 200,000 men and ultimately the senior levies were discharged. Following the debacles in Greece and North Africa a new mobilization began, now focusing mostly on those aged 20 to 25. A similar situation was to be found in Libya; in the first ten days of June 1940 alone, some 67,000 soldiers were hurriedly sent from Italy and by 10 June the army had 11,000 young recruits. In November Superasi reported some 7,000 men aged 31 or more, plus another 76,000 aged 24 to 30; as soldiers in North Africa required the same treatment as any others, a series of discharges was deemed necessary and apparently took place during the summer of 1940, coming to an end with the British offensive in December. In 1941 the Italian army re-mobilized, incorporating soldiers aged 20 to 30; this enabled it to send 86,000 men to Libya during the course of the year, both reinforcements and replacements. On average, the Italian soldier in North Africa was mostly quite young, between 22 and 30, even younger in the unique case of the volunteers of the Giovani Fascisti regiment, who were only 20 or younger. Physical selection for service in the theatre was not strict, soldiers needing to meet only basic requirements such as their teeth being in order or being in reasonable health.

Three main issues relate to Italian soldiers in North Africa: rank, rotation and replacement. The breakdown of ranks in June 1941 shows a clear pattern; officers were 6,965 (5 per cent), NCOs 9,478 (7 per cent), rank and file 120,222 (88 per cent). Detailed breakdown is more revealing; out of

A 20mm Breda 35 gun in an anti-aircraft emplacement manned by artillerymen, probably in Tunisia. They are all wearing the early-style *camiciotto sahariano* along with the model 1933 steel helmet, also crudely painted sand colour, and they are also wearing cross-chest ammunition pouches. (Filippo Cappellano)

a total strength of 61,445 in X and XX Corpo, the combat troops, officers were 3,175 (5 per cent) and NCOs 3,837 (6 per cent), the percentage varying between 5 and 8 per cent within divisions. The same figures in rear-area troops show 1,714 officers (4.7 per cent) and 2,457 NCOs (6.8 per cent), showing an uneven distribution of cadres between the front and the rear. Rotation of personnel added a further problem; up to 1941 this was not much of a problem but after early 1942 it became stringent. Because of the severe strain of life in the desert, in 1941 Superasi suggested rotating personnel after one year of duty in North Africa, but the general staff chose to increase the required period to 24 months at first, then to 36 with at least two months at the front line, eventually reducing it to 34. As early as September 1941, 10,800 men were eligible for rotation, rising to 15,000 in October with a monthly increase of 4,000 men (plus another 3,000 senior levies). In November 1941 Superasi estimated 26,500 men were eligible for rotation, which required 3,000 replacements monthly. Following the start of Operation *Crusader*, rotation was suspended for three months reappearing again in February 1942, when 11,800 men had to be discharged and another 15,000 rotated, mostly serving on the front line.

Provisions were made to send 29,400 replacements at a rate of 2,500 a month, but already in March 1942 requests were made for 43,000 reinforcements and 17,000 replacements, which, with a monthly rate of 10,000, would have taken at least eight months. The situation worsened when figures were revised, now requiring 40,000 reinforcements and 49,000 replacements; since it became clear that the monthly quota of 11,000 Italian soldiers sent to Libya could not be met, in May 1942 the numbers were reduced by cancelling the 5,000 monthly replacements also needed for rotation. In June 1942, after the increased requirement for rotation, which led to shrinking figures, Superasi reported 6,200 men repatriated (3,200 discharged,

A 65/17 infantry gun belonging to 'La Spezia' airlanding division in Tunisia; this rare version of the gun was supplied to the 'La Spezia' division for the planned assault against Malta, in order to make it airborne. The crew members are wearing khaki tropical uniform with woollen socks. (Filippo Cappellano)

An *autocannone* gun portee from a motorized *gruppo autocannoni* (gun portee battalion) during the *Crusader* battle, winter 1941. In this case the 100/17 field gun has been mounted on a Lancia 3 Ro NM diesel-fuelled truck which, although 4x2, proved suitable for the desert. (Filippo Cappellano)

3,000 rotating), with another 11,000 left. On 23 July, after the collapse of the 'Sabratha', Mussolini personally ordered the repatriation of at least 10 men daily, but he was told that, even with increased quotas, by 1 September the figures of those eligible for rotation would rise from 11,000 to 35,000 (including some 10,000 in the divisions). Nevertheless, in August the decision was made to rotate at least 1,000 men monthly, an impossible task given both shortages (10,000 short of established strength) and rotation (14,000 already eligible). In fact, between January and October 1942, 84,000 men were sent to North Africa, both reinforcements (45,000) and replacements (39,000). The latter were badly needed, with Superasi reporting in June 1942 average losses

B TANK HUNTING TRAINING, 'TRENTO' DIVISION, 1942

During the early war years infantry lacked suitable anti-tank weapons, in particular individual weapons that could be carried and manned by a single soldier. The Italian Army, like others, relied initially on anti-tank rifles that, even in 1941, were effective only against light-armoured vehicles. They were too heavy and cumbersome and had too slow a rate of fire to be really effective. Given the delay in developing an anti-tank gun that could replace the now outdated 47mm, the Italian infantry developed (in contrast to German and British forces, which relied more and more on new anti-tank guns) a whole series of close-range, individual anti-tank hand grenades and devices, mostly developed with ingenuity on the field. Already in 1942, infantry was trained using either mock-ups or borrowed M13/40 tanks as seen here, specifically for close-combat, anti-tank tactics; when a tank approached, soldiers had to throw smoke grenades from their dugouts to hinder visibility and hide their approach to the tank as much as possible. Once it was at close range, they leapt out, closing in on the tank and throwing their grenades either against the engine deck or the tracks, to immobilize it. In this scene an infantry lieutenant supervises the training exercise, which has an M13/40 tank under attack by soldiers armed with a training weapon, a wooden stick (broom handle), 20-odd centimetres long, with an SRCM 35 hand grenade attached, trailing smoke. This was the standard hand grenade used for training and was usually reloaded for re-use with the appropriate tools contained in the wooden box shown next to the officer. Also next to the officer are a series of anti-tank grenades and devices that include (from left to right): a British ST grenade, with the explosive in a glass container covered by sticky material and protected by a tin lid; an OTO model 42 grenade; a glass container filled with petrol ignited by the hand grenade on top secured by a metal capsule; an L grenade, made of a simple hand grenade put into a metal container (often a tin can) filled with explosive and secured to a wooden handle; a 'Pazzaglia' bomb, named after the *guastatori* officer who invented it (it was made of a hand grenade secured to a canvas bag filled with explosive); and two 'Molotov' cocktails, one ignited by a hand grenade and the other by a signal flare.

A Breda 30 light machine-gun squad dashing forward in the desert. The standard infantry squad and platoon support weapon, the Breda 30 was hampered by its complicated mechanism and slow rate of fire. (Filippo Cappellano)

of 500–600 infantrymen for each division, 100 men for two Bersaglieri regiments (the third required 400 replacements), 300 artillerymen and 300 tank crews. The army staff put together 3,200 men (including 236 officers and 200 NCOs) in June, and another 1,500 in July; by 7 July more than 4,000 replacements were sent to North Africa by air, but to no avail for on the 11th a new request came for an entire battalion to make good losses suffered in the meantime by the 7° Reggimento Bersaglieri.

Lack of rotation, losses and insufficient replacements meant the Italian soldier in North Africa faced severe strain; combat unit losses between 26 May and 31 July 1942 were 12,000 to 20,000 (only the 979 killed are certain, figures for wounded varied between 6,000 and 11,000, missing from 5,000 to 8,000), plus another 1,000 lost at Alam Halfa. Thus, even after an increase in army strength from January to June of some 11,500, the fact that this had dropped by 1 August by more than 10,000 men clearly shows how overall strength was maintained thanks to reinforcements rather than replacements, which meant the men at the front suffered all the wear and tear of an overextended period of service: a condition that worsened after the creation of the Tunisian bridgehead, with some 60,000 more men sent to North Africa but with practically no hope of relief by rotation.

TRAINING

Military training in Italy started well before the year of duty; young males joined the Fascist youth organization at eight ('Gioventù Italiana del Littorio' or GIL), which was also intended to provide pre-military training. This was limited, however, consisting mostly of weekly meetings and a great deal of physical training. Lessons in theory were given at school between the ages of 13 and 18, with a further two years of tuition at university up to the age of 20. In reality only future substantive officers undertook full training before joining the colours, while others mostly worked on improving their physical fitness. Training under the colours was also limited; emphasis was placed again on physical exercise with soldiers undertaking a series of drills and setting-up exercises daily which, along with labour and long marches held on a regular basis, kept them fit. Actual combat training had many serious shortcomings, being mainly focused at squad and platoon level, with only a few major field exercises being undertaken to improve inter-arms cooperation.

Training was mostly aimed at preparing soldiers to fight in the rugged mountain areas of northern Italy; the social background of the average soldier gave rise to further limitations. Most soldiers came from rural areas, and lacked schooling and technical knowledge and skills, and as a result there were quite serious shortages of drivers and mechanics. Reserve officers, mostly substantive, were promoted by seniority when not on active duty, even though they undertook only theoretical training along with yearly recalls for a short period of duty and training (limited to some 20,000–30,000 reserve officers). Therefore many junior officers up to the rank of captain, or even senior officers up to the rank of major and above, lacked knowledge of even the most recent of the weapons in use.

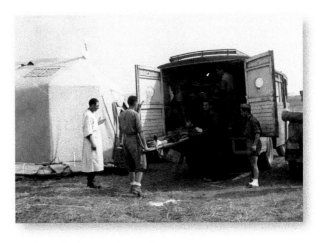

A wounded man is taken to an ambulance in a field hospital in the desert; the lack of motor transport, ambulances in particular, and the fact that most of the field hospitals were located deep in the rear areas meant that often the wounded could not be treated in time. (Ernesto G. Vitetti)

Adequate training was, from the beginning, a serious shortcoming for Italian soldiers in North Africa. In June 1940 Superasi highlighted the difficulty of training troops since they were employed in building fortifications, a situation aggravated in some cases by the lack of weapons and motor vehicles (which was even worse amongst Blackshirt and Libyan units). Following mobilization it was clear that reserve officers, now forming the bulk of first lieutenants and captains, lacked both adequate preparation and an aptitude for command and leadership. With Balbo and Graziani neglecting to improve the training of their troops, Italian soldiers in 1940–41 fell prey to several shortcomings: lack of training for mobile and armoured warfare, in particular anti-tank and reconnaissance, and lack of adequate knowledge of their weapons, resulting in ineffective use of mortars and guns.

Field training in the desert, probably for the planned attack against the Gazala Line. Under cover of a light Breda 30 machine gun, infantry soldiers are removing mines to open a path for the assault. All are wearing *sahariana* jackets or pullover jackets, with model 1933 steel helmets. (Filippo Cappellano)

In 1941 the overall lack of training for the troops and the lack of preparation for the officers were all too clear, and the chief of army staff required the training of the new class of recruits to have a particular emphasis on the use of heavy weapons, particularly anti-tank guns. Actual results must have been disappointing for, that same November, new orders had to be issued asking for improved training and morale of units, once more with an emphasis on the use of anti-tank weapons following the example given by troops in North Africa. As a matter of fact, it was the Italian soldier in North Africa that somehow set the standard, facing a new and unexpected kind of warfare in unfamiliar terrain. In this theatre, training was now a priority and, between the spring and summer of 1941, Superasi created a network of training centres and establishments for new units and for replacements. This included the training centre for infantry and engineers at Barce (initially at Homs), the artillery training centre at El Abiar near Bengasi (plus a training establishment directly subordinated to Superasi), and the tank crew centre, including repair workshops, in the area of Derna, plus specialized schools for communications specialists, motor vehicle drivers and other specialists at Tripoli. The tank crew centre at Derna, formed in June 1941, was made up of an HQ, a storage depot, a supply centre, and a recovery unit including a lorry platoon, one section each for the two medium tank battalions already in the area (VII and VIII), a recovery squad for the five light tank battalions (I to V), and a captured enemy vehicle section. Three repair workshops were set up at Derna, Gazala and near Tobruk, while a four-section replacement training unit was also formed with a strength of 30 officers, 50 NCOs and 340 other ranks. Not much later, 'Ariete's' 'colonna Santamaria' (a task force unit formed around the 8° Reggimento Bersaglieri under the command of Colonnello Santamaria) was disbanded, with a portion of its personnel being sent to the infantry training centre at Barce, the rest being sent back to the unit or to the newly formed Corpo d'Armata Mobile's reconnaissance unit.

This was a necessary step in training not only the soldiers on the spot and their replacements, but also reinforcements; the 'Trieste' division arrived in Libya after a rest and reorganization period spent in Italy, during which only one series of training activities was undertaken. The 'Ariete' tank regiment, at first equipped only with light tanks, was reorganized in Libya between March and August 1941, most of the crews lacking not only experience of

An 88mm anti-aircraft and anti-tank gun battery in the desert with Italian crew, probably in Egypt in 1942 (note the grey-green uniforms and the 91 rifle). The German 88 Flak was supplied to the Italian Army, which used it either in its customary anti-aircraft or anti-tank role, in Italy or in North Africa. (Filippo Cappellano)

the new vehicle but also any knowledge of the tank combat tactics used in the Western Desert. Even the crews of the new medium tank battalions badly needed training for, as recalled by Tenente Enrico Serra of the 132° Reggimento Corazzato, when he joined his unit in December 1941, many tank drivers lacked experience, and gunners had fired only three rounds apiece. Already in February and March 1941 the 'Ariete' division held a series of training exercises aimed at achieving a degree of inter-arms cooperation that eventually enabled it to form the task forces that in April drove into Cyrenaica. Tactics and procedures were changed, according to experience, to suit the requirements of the theatre of war; in April 1941 the 'Trento' division commander gave the order not to abandon non-operational vehicles

Soldiers of the Giovani Fascisti regiment manning an 8mm Breda 37 heavy machine gun in a stone sangar. They are all in shirtsleeves and are wearing black fezes. The feeding of the ammunition clip is clearly visible. (Filippo Cappellano)

(intended to be recovered by the corps recovery units), but rather to create recovery squads following the other units of the division. He also ordered anti-tank guns to be always in combat formation, either while marching or while pausing, ready to deploy to face any threat. Infantry units trained their men too, albeit mostly using old-fashioned methods; the 'Pavia' division, earmarked to take part in the planned assault against Tobruk in the autumn of 1941, had its men in the meantime improving their physical fitness and training for anti-tank warfare with infantry guns and impromptu incendiary devices. Replacements from Italy also underwent the same procedure, with 'Bologna' division's II/39th Battaglione di Fanteria being formed from a replacement division at the infantry training centre at Barce.

Problems surfaced again with reorganization of the 'AS 42' establishments and the arrival of new replacements; on 23 May 1942 XXI Corpo reported that three infantry battalions of the 'Pavia' and 'Brescia' divisions lacked both training and anti-tank weapons, and that three more weeks were required before their use which actually took place a few days later. Early in August 1942 Superasi did complain to the army staff about replacements arriving in Libya so poorly trained that, in spite of the urgent need at the battlefront, they had to be sent to training centres so that they could at least handle their own weapons. It is worth noting that, as early as late February and early March 1942, the army staff agreed to send units already formed according to the new 'AS 42' establishments to Libya, their men trained and led by skilled officers. In spite of renewed interest that led the army staff in 1942 to improve training to make good the lack of anti-tank weapons, this problem seemed deeply rooted, mostly because of sheer lack of ammunition. Early in 1942 infantry had only 35 rounds for training with the 47/32 gun, 55 with the 20mm Breda anti-aircraft gun, and 60 with the 65/17 infantry gun. Tanks and armoured car crews had only five to eight rounds to practise with their main gun and, from June 1942, the new levy of draftees had only the unused rounds left behind by their predecessors to train with.

In 1942 the Italian soldier in North Africa was to face two main training issues: improving firing drills and anti-tank combat training, in order to make up for the shortcomings of their weapons. Both reinforcements and replacements arriving in North Africa would start with firing drills, but it was not long before difficulties arose there too; as early as April 1942 it was no longer possible to supply armour-piercing rounds for the 75mm and the 88mm guns supplied by the Germans, and in June the supplies of 47/32 and 65/17 hollow charge rounds were exhausted. Overall lack of ammunition meant that not all the reinforcements and replacements could be properly trained, and it is therefore not surprising that in autumn 1942 local commanders preferred to strip the 'Pistoia' and armoured 'Centauro' divisions of their assets to reinforce the overstrained, but battle-hardened and properly trained, divisions at Alamein. The exception to this rule, the deployment at the battlefront of the 'Folgore' paratrooper division, one of the best-trained units along with 'La Spezia' division (both had been formed and trained for the planned assault against Malta), does suggest that properly trained Italian soldiers, even when not yet tested in battle, could perform adequately, which the men of the 'Folgore' did in October 1942.

Anti-tank training was badly needed in 1942 because Italian weapons, now largely outdated, would still have some degree of effectiveness on the battlefield if used at very short range. Basically the Italians aimed now at immobilizing the enemy tanks either with their anti-tank guns or with improvised throwing devices, both requiring skilled and well-trained soldiers. Training emphasized close combat (300m or less and down to 20–30m, where even Italian weapons were effective) and the knowledge and use of all available weapons, including impromptu ones. Field manuals and posters showing enemy vehicles and their 'weak points' were circulated, and soldiers were taught that tanks were not a mighty, invulnerable enemy, but just required a good deal of stamina and courage in order to combat them. On the other hand this kind of training was not without consequences; while the Germans and the British used long-range weapons, the fact that Italians fought better at very close range required different tactics. Thus, while others would look for dominant features of the landscape and clear fields of fire, the Italians were taught to deploy in narrower areas, preferably those 'forced passages' the enemy tanks had to use. Obviously, Italian soldiers' training for defence improved, while efficacy in attack would be reduced.

Officers arriving in North Africa faced other problems, such as orientation and discipline while marching (particularly the need to assess where they were and to reach their assigned positions in the shortest possible time). Drivers had to be trained too, particularly new drivers, all too often without driving licences and

Bersaglieri firing an 8mm Breda 37 heavy machine gun from the ruins of a house. Note how, apart from the officer on the right, all are wearing a *camiciotto sahariano*; the two on the left also have camouflage on their helmets, but retain the characteristic cockerel feathers.
(Filippo Cappellano)

yet, in spite of their lack of driving skill and experience, they were needed to keep the flow of supplies going. Lack of fuel was not the only factor that hampered proper training in the field of mobile warfare, which remained one of the weaknesses of Italian soldiers in North Africa; even in 1942 an Italian mobile division could travel at only 7km/h on good terrain, compared with the 20km/h or more of a German division. Reaching the Alamein front the men of the 'Littorio' armoured division lacked navigational instruments and detailed maps, the few available being not only inaccurate but also on different scales. It is no wonder that the division was able to march only widely dispersed on the terrain, and at a speed of only 5km/h.

Training of replacements became increasingly difficult in late 1942, with only 245 officers and 2,680 other ranks being sent to the front in October. By 15 December there were more than 9,000 men (infantry 2,999, tank crews 2,888, and artillery 4,229) available in training centres, which by November had formed one provisional battalion and one company. Thanks to these men it was possible to replenish the 'Trieste' division, merging most of the remnants from El Alamein, eventually providing the backbone of the new 1st army in Tunisia that could rely on a large number of trained, battle-hardened and seasoned veterans well determined to defend the last African stronghold.

Men of the San Marco marine regiment in Tunisia, manning a Breda 37 heavy machine gun. Although the army was the main fighting force in North Africa, land forces from the navy and the air force (and the Fascist militia as well) also fought there. (Filippo Cappellano)

APPEARANCE AND EQUIPMENT

The standard Italian army uniform, introduced in the mid-1930s, included a side cap and a new steel helmet, an open-collar jacket with matching trousers worn with either riding boots (officers) or puttees and marching boots (other ranks). The jacket was worn with shirt and tie, the colour of the collar changing according to the corps and branch of service. It had four pleated pockets with flaps, two on the breast and two at the waist, and was fastened at the front by four buttons and a fabric belt. Officers' uniforms were made of high-quality fabric, often tailor-made, trousers having two black lines along the seam, sewn with the colour of the branch of service. Other ranks wore breeches-style trousers, reaching just below the knees, together with puttees. Officers wore a peaked cap or *bustina*, a side cap that differed from that of other ranks in cut and quality. A series of different styles of headgear was in use for different conditions; all *Alpini* wore their peculiar hat regardless of rank (with slight differences), while other ranks *Bersaglieri* wore their red fez with blue tassel on duty (the Giovani Fascisti regiment wore a similar hat in black). Shirts were initially made of heavy fabric, open at the neck and chest and, before the war, it was customary to use a kind of polo shirt with a zip fastening at the front. An overcoat was worn over the uniform in wintertime, sometimes replaced by a cape, worn (mostly on official duty) by the *Alpini* and the *Bersaglieri*.

In 1935 a new tropical uniform was introduced on a wide scale when Italy started her war against Ethiopia, with the same cut as the European version, made of greenish-khaki fabric (sometimes cotton); it included a jacket worn over a shirt, and long trousers tucked into ankle-boots (paratrooper style). The jacket was open at the neck and had four pleated pockets with flaps like the European version, the only difference being the cuff, which was decorated with an upward-pointing triangle motif. Long trousers and boots, being too expensive, were discarded when the army mobilized in 1939 in favour of greenish-khaki cloth breeches, again worn with grey-green European puttees and brown (rather than black) boots. From June 1940 other details changed; European uniforms lost their coloured collars, now grey-green like the rest of the jacket, officers' trousers lost their black lines along the seam, while the use of a tie was officially prohibited. Tropical uniforms also underwent changes, other than the introduction of breeches, the cuffs being simplified by having a round motif. Two items

MAGGIORE, 32° REGGIMENTO CARRI, DIVISIONE 'ARIETE', 1942

This major from the 32° Reggimento Carri, Divisione 'Ariete' is wearing the uniform most commonly used by Italian officers in North Africa, a *sahariana* jacket with its characteristic pleated breast pocket and 'winged' flaps. This very comfortable jacket was one of the favourite items, even amongst German officers. It was worn either with or without a cotton shirt. The peaked cap, a '*bustina 42*' (*bustina* being Italian for side cap), was a modified version of the side cap inspired by the German field cap. On it were both an embroidered tank corps badge **(1)**, (the metal version) and, on the left-hand side, a rank badge, which was also worn on the shoulder straps; it was commonly used with tropical uniforms and made of black board (with golden thread all round, as required by rank, along with the star) over a backing of the arm of service colour, in this case red for infantry (the tank corps badge is also worn on the straps). The actual tank corps colours were red and blue, the tank units belonging to the infantry and forming its mechanized branch (blue is the colour of the transport corps). His only weapon is a 9mm Beretta 34 pistol. On his chest, above the ribbons and to the right, this veteran officer wears the badge for officers who had attended war school courses (*scuola di guerra*, in practice staff courses) and, to the left, a war merit promotion badge; on his right arm he also has a war wound badge. On the left pocket is the newly issued metal badge for tank crews **(2)**, carrying the tank corps motto 'iron hull, iron hearts'. Medal ribbons include (left to right) the cross for military valour, *croce di guerra al valor militare* **(3)**, the order of the crown of Italy, the campaign medal for the war against Ethiopia in 1935–36 **(6)**, bearing on top the inscription 'Eastern Africa' and, below, Mussolini's motto 'many enemies, much honour', the Spanish Civil War campaign medal, the World War II campaign medal and the Spanish Civil War volunteers medal. The World War II campaign medal **(5)**, created in late 1941, was designed complete with bars only after the war, one for each war year; up to then only the ribbon was worn, with a star for each year. Also shown are the German-Italian North Africa campaign medal **(4)** and the 'Ariete' division commemorative medal **(7)** for the spring 1941 Cyrenaica campaign.

A 20mm Breda 35 gun in a desert emplacement with a *Bersaglieri* crew, probably 1942 (note the *camiciotto sahariano* worn by these men). Although a fine anti-aircraft weapon, the Breda 35 was also intended for use as an anti-tank gun, for which it was not effective. Note the 9mm Beretta 38 MP worn by the *Bersagliere* on the left. (Filippo Cappellano)

introduced in the mid-1930s did remain in use, becoming more and more popular: the tropical pith helmet or topee, officers sometimes wearing British-style versions ('Aden'), and the *sahariana* jacket. This, reserved for officers, was characterized by a shirt-style cut, with buttons at the collar and cuffs and, in particular, by the peculiar shape of the upper portion round the chest and the back, which had a 'winged' style that, at the front, also formed the pocket flaps for the two pleated chest pockets (there were two more pockets, without pleats, at the waist). Tied at the waist by a fabric belt and usually produced in fine-quality cotton, this became so popular it turned into an all-purpose garment, officers (who also used to order it tailor-made) wearing it on all occasions, even formal.

In 1939–40 the ministry of the colonies introduced a new-model jacket for use by Libyan soldiers, with two different cuts; called *camiciotto sahariano* (shirt-like *sahariana*), it was available either as a simple jacket open at the front and cut in the same style as the *sahariana*, apart from the upper winged portion, or as a pullover jacket open only at the neck and the chest, with two large slits on both sides at the bottom for ease of wearing and removal. Both had collar and cuffs fastened with buttons, two pleated pockets on the chest with flaps and two more pockets at the waist (the first

A typical dugout in the desert, in this case for a Breda 30 light machine-gun team (note how the two crew members are holding a 91 rifle with foldable bayonet). The dugout was often just a simple shallow hole camouflaged by a net, therefore it could be detected only at very close range. (Filippo Cappellano)

type did not have pleats, unlike the second type; both had flaps) and both had a fabric belt around the waist. Tested at first by the army soldiers during field exercises held in 1938, it was not introduced into use until later in the war. Therefore, the Italian soldiers in Libya in 1939–40 were supplied either with the new- or old-style tropical uniform or, in many cases, with the European grey-green uniform, still quite useful, especially in winter, although worn with a tropical pith helmet (a greenish-khaki cloth version of the side cap was also produced). The grey fatigue uniform was used too, along with the new tropical

overcoat made of greenish-khaki wool and of the same cut as the grey-green version, double breasted and with a large collar plus two large pockets at the sides.

A motorized column of the 9º Reggimento Bersaglieri of the 'Trieste' infantry division; only a few Italian units were motorized, and then only with trucks. Note that all are wearing tropical pith helmets and *camiciotto sahariano*, and the stretcher-bearer has a Red Cross armband. (Filippo Cappellano)

Shortages of stock and supplies, even field uniforms and equipment, were typical of the life of Italian soldiers in North Africa; in July 1940 Superasi quartermaster reported an overall shortage of 50,000 camouflaged tent quarters (widely used in Libya), 50,000 greenish-khaki uniforms, and 200,000 pairs of boots, all items needed to be supplied from Italy since local production was non-existent. A widespread lack of the model 1933 steel helmets seems to have plagued Italian soldiers in North Africa, for this seems to be rarely worn when not in combat, even though it is undeniable that the tropical pith helmet was certainly preferred on many occasions. Following the example of British and German soldiers, and given shortages in available stock, from 1941 changes were introduced in the uniforms of Italian soldiers as well. The *camiciotto sahariano* was distributed both to those already in Libya and to those being moved there, while the use of shorts was introduced, both being made official in July. Further improvements were considered, including long trousers and ankle-boots, but never came into being.

In the summer of 1941 the uniform of the Italian soldier in North Africa included a *camiciotto sahariano* jacket made of greenish-khaki fabric worn with a shirt of the same colour, greenish-khaki shorts (new underpants were also supplied), cotton or woollen socks sometimes replacing the puttees, still largely used with breeches, tropical pith helmet and greenish-khaki side cap. A new model of headgear was introduced, in effect a visored field cap resembling the old-style side cap but adapted, following the model of the German visored field cap; called *bustina modello 42* (model 42 side cap, characterized by foldable neck and ear protection, like the old-style side cap, but with a visor added), this became a much-appreciated and widely used item. Sand protection goggles, of a different type and quality, a two-litre new canteen, two belly bands (cloth or woollen bands worn around the belly to protect from gastrointestinal diseases, until then only one had been distributed), new off-duty shoes, and a new model of tactical haversack were also distributed. The old-style breeches, usually worn with grey-green puttees (also worn with shorts), did remain in use, although soldiers proved keener on using shorts or, facing a shortage of those, on obtaining their

A group of *Bersaglieri* mounted on motorcycles, attacking enemy positions in a village in Tunisia. All are armed with the 6.5mm 91 rifle, and all are wearing model 1933 steel helmets with grey-green jackets over khaki trousers. (Filippo Cappellano)

own, preferably pressing into service whatever piece of captured enemy uniform and equipment they could get hold of. This practice became widespread after the seizure of Tobruk in June 1942 and the looting of its storage, with Italian soldiers widely using British-made shirts and boots (plus jackets and shorts), although British tropical pith helmets were not much appreciated.

Although changes introduced to the uniform of the Italian soldier in North Africa finally met the requirements of this theatre of war, old-style and grey-green uniforms were still largely used. Shortages were, as usual, one of the reasons; in January 1942 the army store in Tripoli reported an overall shortage of 408,000 shirts (450,000 were required for a three-month period), 24,500 shorts (163,000 required), 10,500 two-litre canteens (26,000 required), 1,500 tank crew overalls (1,500 required), 25,000 pairs of sandals (25,000 required), along with a shortage of 300,000 pairs of lapel badges. The use of the grey-green uniform, or parts of it, thus became necessary, and not only during the winter; many soldiers sent to Libya still wore it, and stocks were sent to Tripoli from May 1942. In November 1942 the use of the grey-green uniform was sanctioned for soldiers sent to North Africa, although the same month the creation of the Tunisian bridgehead and the subsequent withdrawal to that area saw the end of the widespread use of tropical uniforms. In fact the last months of the war in North Africa saw Italian soldiers mostly wearing the grey-green uniform, or a mixture of grey-green and greenish-khaki tropical uniforms (sometimes with the addition of further protective clothing such as windcheaters), while in most cases the traditional tropical pith helmet was discarded in preference to the more practical model 1933 steel helmet, the 42 visored field cap being still largely in use. On the other hand, the uniforms used by tank crews and other troops such as drivers did remain unchanged, with their characteristic blue overalls and (especially for the tank crews) the large, and much-needed, protective leather helmet.

Overall shortage of uniforms, the mixture of different versions (including those captured from the enemy) and the variety of climates characterizing the different areas of the theatre led to a certain relaxed attitude toward dressing, similar to their German counterparts (along with a certain slackening of military standards). This was to the great annoyance of their commanders who repeatedly complained of the many violations to norms and practices and issued several detailed orders, all too often largely ignored. If this attitude was understandable, even largely tolerated, for the soldiers at the front, the same was not true for those who served in the rear, particularly at Tripoli. Here complaints were made, for example, about the widespread wearing of shirt lapels over jackets. Obviously, the concerns of those at the front were quite different; here soldiers not only suffered from lack of uniforms (and the difficulty of washing them), but also from inadequate equipment and weapons.

Officers mostly used the standard 'Sam Browne' style belt with sling, together with the accompanying pistol holster, map and compass case; NCOs and rank and file were equipped with a small leather belt suspended around the neck by a small sling used to support two ammunition pouches. Normally painted grey-green to match the European uniform, but often worn in their natural brown leather colour, these were neither comfortable nor practical, the leather unavoidably cracking from contact with the perspiration of the owner. Slightly better were the cross-chest pouches, mostly for soldiers belonging to motorized and mechanized units (but also used, whenever possible, by all others), also made of brown leather. Other pieces of equipment included the bayonet, worn with its scabbard and frog on the belt, the canvas gas-mask bag (widely worn in North Africa), the one- or two-litre aluminium canteen with fabric cover, and the canvas bread bag, all too often used, particularly during combat, to carry hand grenades. A small haversack was also used, often with a rolled blanket or rolled camouflage tent quarter tied to it (or even both, one on top of the other).

Individual weapons were in some cases inferior to those of the other armies; the standard pistol was the semi-automatic 9mm Beretta 34, although Glisenti revolvers and the old Bodeo pistols were also used. The Italian rifle was the 6.5mm Carcano model 1891, also available in 7.35mm calibre. There were three versions: standard; short musket with a fixed, foldable bayonet; and simple musket – designated 'for special troops' (different varieties of bayonets were also used). With a six-round magazine, the rifle had a smaller calibre and a relative lack of power, although its accuracy was appreciated. The standard light machine gun was more troublesome; the 6.5mm Breda 30 (initially an automatic rifle, then a light machine gun) was greatly hampered by the oil pump needed to lubricate its rounds, and by the fixed 20-round magazine that made for complicated reloading. Effective at

An Italian soldier in the desert posing with one of the few examples of the 9mm Beretta 38 MP issued to the troops in 1942, holding it in a way unsuitable for firing. Mostly the 'Folgore' paratroopers, the *Bersaglieri* and the Giovani Fascisti regiment were supplied with the Beretta 38 MP in North Africa. (Filippo Cappellano)

Mine detector being tested in Egypt in 1942, in this case an experimental example produced in Libya. Both soldiers are wearing their grey-green European uniform, including a side cap because of the lack of tropical uniforms. (Filippo Cappellano)

M13/40 medium tanks moving in the desert in open formation, almost certainly belonging to the 'Ariete' armoured division. The M13/40 and M14/41 tanks were the main Italian battle tanks in the Western Desert in 1940–42. (Filippo Cappellano)

a range of some 500m, it was excessively delicate and very much inclined to jam. Much better were the standard heavy machine guns, the 8mm Breda 37 and Fiat-Revelli 35; both the first, magazine feed (20 rounds), and the second, belt feed (50 to 100 rounds), had a slow rate of fire (200, 250 up to 350 rounds per minute) compared with their weight (19.4kg and 17kg). The light 45mm Brixia 35 mortar was an excessively complicated weapon firing a very light grenade (480g) with just 70g of explosive, at 500m, while the 81mm model 35 mortar was quite an effective weapon firing a 3.3kg–6.6kg grenade up to 1,100m. Only a few machine pistols, the 9mm Beretta 38, were used to equip Italian soldiers in North Africa in 1942, mostly the Giovani Fascisti and the paratroopers (the weapon entered army use in 1941, mass production starting in 1942). Italian hand grenades (OTO, Breda and SRCM) were, generally speaking, too lightweight to be effective.

Anti-tank weapons were the Italian soldiers' real Achilles heel; the standard 47/32 gun was intended for anti-tank use along with the anti-aircraft 20mm Breda 35 gun, both being already outdated in 1940. Apart from makeshift solutions like the development of various kinds of explosive and incendiary grenades, the only anti-tank weapons supplied to the Italian soldiers in North Africa were the anti-tank rifles. These included the 20mm, Swiss-made Solothurn and the German-supplied (Polish-made) 7.92mm model 35, although large numbers of the captured British Boys anti-tank rifles were also pressed into Italian use. Basically, the problem with the 47/32 anti-tank gun was that it had been conceived for use in mountain warfare; it was therefore intended to be broken down for mule transport (it weighed 78.2kg), which made its use in the desert quite awkward since the gun was unsuitable for towing, soldiers having to pull it. Guns were mostly carried aboard lorries, when not actually mounted on them for use as portees, a popular solution in North Africa. Needless to say, this solution clashed with the shortage of motor vehicles, and in 1940 the 'Cirene' division had to dismantle all its portees to hand the lorries back to supply.

Having faced heavy tanks such as the Matilda in 1940 the Italians mainly focused on the development of the 90mm anti-tank/anti-aircraft gun, which was very effective compared with the German 88mm. This is possibly the reason for the lack of development of a medium-sized anti-tank gun like the British 17-pdr or the German 75mm PAK, which, in any case, made their appearance only in late 1942 to early 1943.

ON CAMPAIGN

The problems common to every soldier fighting in North Africa were environment and climate. These would change, sometimes dramatically, from area to area and from time to time; Cyrenaica in winter offered a milder climate with occasional rain, while summer in Egypt was like a dry furnace, and Tunisia was more like a Mediterranean country. Nevertheless, some factors were common to almost all places: the sand, the intense heat during the day and the freezing cold at night, the swarms of insects, the almost inevitable consequences of both terrain and logistics. In consequence soldiers from both sides experienced the following problems at least once during the campaign: hunger, thirst, the constant need for a bath and a change of clothes, and their being far away from home and from their loved ones. Sometimes the simple material conditions of everyday life would affect soldiers' morale more than victory or defeat, and such factors were influenced by the way each individual army dealt with the welfare of its own troops.

Time for coffee. Italian soldiers in North Africa were not supplied with shorts until the summer of 1941 and this particular item of clothing was not really appreciated by senior officers, who were concerned about a possible lowering of standards. Judging by this photo their concern was justified. (Ernesto G. Vitetti)

The Italian army lagged behind others in this respect, for several reasons; firstly, there was the gulf that all too often divided officers and soldiers. In a society still largely rural and characterized by a rigid class system, those who had the chance to become officers were either part of the urban mid-upper classes or they belonged to the gentry and, as such, had very little in common with their soldiers. These would in most cases come from rural areas, still largely experiencing varying degrees of poverty and widespread illiteracy (many spoke and understood only local dialects), and from large families. Italian officers were often accused of showing little, if any, interest in their subordinates, and this had unavoidable consequences for their welfare and morale. There were exceptions of course, although this indifference was typical. Secondly, one ought to also consider the logistical difficulty Italians (and Germans as well) faced in North Africa; almost everything had to be brought in from Italian harbours and, when supplies reached Tripoli, they had to be transported from Libyan harbours all the way down to the front line, mostly by road. The single tarmac road, the 'via Balbia', stretched for some 700-odd kilometres from Tripoli to El Agheila and, from there, for another 700-odd kilometres to Tobruk. Distances dramatically increased to Egypt; more than 1,500km divided Tripoli from Sollum, with another 370km between Sollum and El Alamein, making a total of about 1,900km between Tripoli and El Alamein.

In some cases supplies were moved via coastal shipping to Tobruk and Matruh, but during most of the campaign Italian troops suffered from the

 ATTACKING THE GAZALA LINE, 'BRESCIA' DIVISION, 1942

One of the least-known aspects of the war in the Western Desert is the contribution given to the Panzer Armee Afrika by Italian infantry units, widely employed to secure defence lines or, as in the case of operations against the Gazala Line in May–June 1942, to attack enemy positions while the armoured and motorized units swung behind them. After spring 1941 there were four Italian infantry divisions deployed around Tobruk fortress and at the Sollum–Halfaya Pass position, which became five when the motorized 'Trento' was transformed into an infantry division. In 1942 the 'Sabratha' division joined in, only to be destroyed at El Alamein in July. All these divisions were destroyed at El Alamein in October–November 1942. The two infantry regiments formed the bulk of an infantry division, with the companies forming the bulk of their three battalions. Three rifle platoons (plus HQ and support) formed the assault elements of a rifle company each with two rifle squads of an established strength of 18 men including the squad commander and his vice. The squads had two separate components: the machine-gun group and the rifle group, the former with two machine-gun teams of four men each and the latter with nine riflemen. Each machine-gun team was supposed to have a leader, one machine-gunner, and two ammunition carriers but, in practice, given the shortage of manpower, they included only three with the leader himself acting as an ammunition carrier. One of the ways to deploy the squad for attack was to have the two machine-gun teams on both wings, while at the centre the commander and his vice led the rifle group to attack, all too often well short of its established strength. The leader, usually a staff sergeant, is positioned here between the machine gun on the left wing and the rifle group, which is led by his vice (a sergeant, the machine-gun squad being led by a lance corporal). Under artillery fire, and trying to take advantage of a breach in the barbed-wire defences, the leading riflemen are advancing under cover from the other riflemen and the machine guns. Firepower was one of the main shortages of the Italian infantry, for there were no machine pistols for the squad leaders and riflemen were armed with only one of the available versions of the 6.5mm 91 Carcano rifle.

A *guastatori* platoon ready for inspection. The *guastatori* (assault engineers) were special forces trained to attack enemy-fortified positions such as Tobruk. On the ground, right in front of the *guastatori*, is a collection of various items including Bangalore tubes and smoke grenades. (Ernesto G. Vitetti)

A German-built 150mm heavy field howitzer 18 which, acquired by the Italian army and used to equip some artillery battalions, was known as the 149/28 gun. The crew is wearing the 1940 tropical uniform including old-style side caps, apart from the sergeant who is wearing the new model 1942. (Ernesto G. Vitetti)

difficulties of the supply system; because of the shortage of motor vehicles, the army adopted centralization and since October 1940 most of the available vehicles had been grouped into two large motor vehicle pools, at the disposal of Superasi and of Tenth Army. The situation hardly changed in 1941–42 but rather worsened, with about one-third of the already-scarce Italian motor transport pool always in need of repair, which is not surprising considering that lorries covered the above-mentioned distances with daily legs of at least 250–300km. One of the consequences was the practical impossibility of establishing supply pools, particularly for divisions that were supplied directly by the Superasi quartermaster. Shortage of vehicles and rigid centralization often meant that it was logistically impossible to keep up with the basic quantity of supplies, particularly food and ammunition. In other words, Italian units were well supplied when the front was static, but greatly suffered when moving, especially on the advance.

Influenced by these factors, the life of Italian soldiers at the front was not particularly easy, as revealed by a screening of postal censorship. After the advance into Cyrenaica and the battles fought at Tobruk and Sollum, in summer 1941 Italian soldiers suffered greatly from fatigue and low morale, mostly on account of the intense heat and poor conditions, including poor standards of hygiene caused by shortage of water. Morale improved in late July thanks to the first instances of leave and the start of an albeit limited rotation and also because food dramatically improved. Until then logistical difficulty had prevented soldiers from being properly fed, but when the front stabilized, supplies were brought forward and, thanks to the time spent by some units in rest areas, soldiers could eat and recover (although complaints were still made about the mutton and a shortage of lemons). As early as August restrictions

imposed on rotation and leave, and widespread fears about the favouritism shown by officers when granting leave, lowered morale, along with worsening food and water supplies, irregular wages and poor postal service. On the other hand soldiers did welcome the new tropical uniforms (not always available). However, low morale and apparent long-term fatigue amongst the troops were also caused by the scant interest officers showed towards their subordinates. Fatigue particularly afflicted the units surrounding Tobruk, with many complaints about lack of replacements, while the elite units ('Trieste', 'Trento', 'Ariete' divisions, the Giovani Fascisti regiment) had excellent morale. Improved supplies and overall conditions enabled recovery and, by November 1941, even the infantry

A wounded RAF pilot is taken to an Italian field hospital to be treated. The group of Italian soldiers, wearing a mixture of grey-green and tropical uniforms including overcoats (and cloth helmet covers), watch with curiosity. (Ernesto G. Vitetti)

divisions showed better spirit, in spite of the constant complaints about lack of rotation and leave, and the many problems with the postal service (letters and packages often being tampered with).

In January 1942, after the *Crusader* battle, the long period of duty in North Africa was still the main cause of complaint; many units had already spent more than one and a half years there, mostly at the front line, while the disruption of supplies once again brought the issues of food, water and postal supply to the fore. In spring the situation improved again, and in June 1942 the seizure of Tobruk and the apparently victorious march into Egypt pushed morale to a high point. Complaints about lack of leave and rotation decreased, the soldiers now being happy to take part in the 'big show'. Even the gulf between officers and other ranks was reduced, to a certain extent. Failure at El Alamein did not change the overall situation; in late September 1942 Italian soldiers in Egypt were now united by a previously unknown degree of camaraderie and *esprit de corps*, which was further improved by the deployment of the 'Folgore' parachute division.

Complaints were still made on a large scale about lack of rotation and leave, but attention focused now on war dodgers and profiteers at home, and on the increasingly difficult situation families and relatives had to face, including scarcity of food and enemy air raids in Italy, along with a series of problems with payment of allowances to families of serving soldiers. Difficulties with supplies, and related complaints about food and the postal service continued, yet some men would use the post to send coffee powder, sugar and even matches back home in envelopes. By mid-October 1942 the situation had not changed very much; many soldiers complained about the long period of duty in the area (some had spent as much as 44 months in North Africa), and the lack of rotation and leave, mostly because of their desire to see their families again. Comparisons between their own weapons and those available to the enemy affected morale as well, as they were faced with decisive improvements in British weapons.

In December, after the battle of El Alamein, Italian soldiers were shaken by the defeat and retreat but those who managed to withdraw still showed confidence and willingness to fight, thanks mostly to their *esprit de corps*. Morale was affected, however, and men did show fatigue and war weariness, particularly because of the lack of rotation and leave, which apparently kept the 'same guys' at the front line, while others enjoyed the comforts of being in the rearguard. Eventually, many developed a clearer picture of the situation; this time taking the road back did not mean that they came closer to home, but closer to the last stand.

Several difficulties were common to both Afrika Korps and Eighth Army soldiers, but the Italians clearly suffered from certain specific problems. Rotation and leave were the first; ideally soldiers should have spent no more than two weeks in combat before then receiving a few days of rest, eventually rotating back home after no more than 400 days, before exhaustion and weariness exacted their toll. In the Western Desert the lack of a front line meant that troops did not often need to be rotated from the front to the rear, apart from the notable exceptions of Tobruk, the Gazala Line and El Alamein. Nevertheless, Eighth Army had divisions that enjoyed long periods of rest, in rear areas such as Alexandria, Cairo or Palestine after combat, a luxury no Axis unit ever enjoyed. For example, after defending the Tobruk fortress for 130 days, the men of the 9th Australian Division showed clear signs of fatigue and exhaustion; from mid-August 1941 the division was relieved (first one half, then the other, in September and October), not to be back in action before July 1942. In contrast, Italian infantry divisions would lay siege to Tobruk without a break from April and May through to December 1941,

REST TIME AT BENGHAZI, 1941

For most of 1941 Benghazi was the ideal rest area for Axis troops, right behind the front, its shops back in business after the town had been seized again in April 1941, and with the *dopolavoro* having organized its armed forces' recuperation and help centres, also working as fully licensed canteens. The *dopolavoro* (literally meaning 'after work') was in fact a kind of workers' club, organized by the Fascist party (Partito Nazionale Fascista, PNF) involved with various working groups in Italy and also the armed forces. For soldiers at the front it not only managed canteens, but also (amongst other things) organized travelling libraries, events and shows. Soldiers either travelling to the front, mostly from the corps of transport bringing supplies from Tripoli, or back for a period of rest could thus enjoy much-needed relaxation, such as this sergeant major and major of the transport corps (*motorizzazione*), who are enjoying some *vino* while listening to the radio. The former wears an overall (very much like those used by tank crews) and the cross-belt pouches normally issued to soldiers of motorized or mounted units, while the latter simply wears a tropical uniform with a *sahariana* jacket. Close to them is a *Bersaglieri* corporal, wearing a *camiciotto sahariano* pullover jacket with shorts (recently introduced) and puttees, and typical red fez with blue tassel worn by the *Bersaglieri* while off duty. Benghazi and other towns in Libya, as well as the 'via Balbia' (Balbo's Road, the tarmacadam road running along the coastline), were patrolled by mixed Italian-German military police units, a necessity given the presence of both Italian and German soldiers. Here one of these patrols, led by an *appuntato* (lance corporal) of the *carabinieri* wearing the tropical version of the visored cap with the *carabinieri*'s flaming grenade in metal and the characteristic lapel badges, is patrolling the streets – the patrol consists of one Italian *carabiniere* and one German *Feldgendarm*. The former wears the *camiciotto sahariano* with the *carabinieri* badges and insignias, the latter (a *Feldwebel*, warrant officer) simply wears a shirt with shorts and the tropical field cap. On his chest he sports a typical *Feldgendarmerie* (military police) gorget, and is armed with an MP 40 9mm machine pistol. The Libyan soldier to the side is wearing the same uniform as the Italians, apart from a characteristic *tachia* red fez and the red and white sash of the infantry depot units, and sandals.

P. N. F.
DOPOLAVORO FORZE ARMATE
POSTO DI RISTORO ED ASSISTENZA MILITARI
SPACCIO.KANTINE

Refuelling in the desert. An Italian supply column, made up of Italian (first and third from the right are two Fiat/Spa TL 37 4x4s, second from the right an Oto Melara 4x2 lorry) and captured British lorries, in the desert. Worth noting, at least two of the Italian soldiers are wearing British battledress. (Filippo Cappellano)

when they withdrew, only to be back at the front line the following February, and back in action less than five months later (mechanized units were in action almost constantly).

Lack of rotation from the front to the rear was not compensated by leave and rotation back home for individual soldiers, another problem common to all armies. Ideally Italian soldiers should have been granted leave to the rear to areas such as Tripoli but this was not possible on a large scale given the lack of transport. Even rotation back home was not possible, as we have seen, although the army acknowledged that after 24 months spent in North Africa in a combat unit both the health of the soldiers and the effectiveness of the units were undermined. Yet this timescale had been increased to 36 months (two of those months at the front) because of a shortage of replacements, although it was eventually reduced to 34. In actual practice this was more of

Strongpoint of the 'La Spezia' division in Tunisia, with a Breda 37 heavy machine gun in the foreground. The photo shows the typical arrangement of these strongpoints, the main gun position and the zigzagging trenches used by the infantry. (Ernesto G. Vitetti)

a promise than a reality and in most cases restricted to a small elite (officers or those in the rear). Leave back home could be granted only for marriages, to undertake university examinations and to take part in selection for national or civil service. Rarer were the cases of leave granted in recognition of heroic deeds, usually the sort of deeds for which one was awarded a medal.

This system caused a great deal of resentment and complaint; officers who had left behind families and jobs could not understand why younger colleagues should be entitled to leave for those same reasons and this resulted in a strict limit being imposed on leave granted for reasons other than marriage. Marriage seemed to be the only chance of getting a ticket back home and it was not unusual for soldiers to write to their parents asking them to find 'a wife of any kind'. Eventually, most of those who made their way back to Italy were either wounded or sick, leaving most of the others behind with their desire to see their nearest and dearest again.

The typical 'barber shop' improvised by the most skilled soldier of the unit, in this case an assault *Arditi* (as shown by the badge on their left arms). Although Italian fashion required long oiled hair, a radical haircut was required at the front. (Ernesto G. Vitetti)

Facing the impossibility of rotating units from the front or individuals back home, in July 1941 Superasi ordered that every division should create a rest camp near to logistic centres or elsewhere close to the sea in order to enable soldiers to enjoy a period of rest. This was limited to no more than ten days plus travel, and periods of rest had to be granted to small units (no smaller than a squad or a company), not individual soldiers unless sick or wounded. Each one of these camps, (those of 'Ariete' and 'Trento' divisions were at Ain El Gazala, that of 'Trieste' at Berta village, that of 'Brescia' at Derna, plus there were two others at Miani village and near Homs) included an officers' mess, increased food rations for both NCOs and rank and file, newspapers, magazines, books, and radio sets. Another solution was the use of military brothels, although not on a large scale. After the advance into Egypt in 1942, with the Italian units now having many long-serving veterans and the impossibility of re-organizing these camps, the situation unavoidably worsened.

Food rations also affected soldiers' morale and health; not until December 1940 were rations for the soldiers in Libya different from those serving at home, with further distinctions made between those at the front and those in the rear. Soldiers in Cyrenaica had a daily ration including 700g of bread, 200g of pasta or 170g of rice, 250g of meat (which could be replaced once or twice a week with canned tuna), 50g of pulses or 100g of potatoes, 10g of coffee, 15g of sugar, 10g of lard or olive oil, 10g of tomato purée, 10g of cheese and 4g of wine. Soldiers were also paid 30 centimes a day to improve their rations, hardly of much use where they were based. Luxuries included 35 cigarettes per week (of the poorer quality), with the possibility of purchasing 35 then 70 more, 30g of chocolate, 50g of marmalade and 3g of spirits. In June 1941 an extra allowance was given for 20g of pasta, 15g of sugar and 10g of surrogate coffee, with the surrogate eventually replacing real coffee once and for all in January 1942.

All too often, reality was very different from intended rations; wood-fuelled bakeries also needed motor transport, with the result that in many cases preserved food replaced fresh. This caused other problems for, from 1941, cans had been produced with reduced quantities of tin, which resulted in rusting and the deterioration of their contents (mostly meat – unsatisfactory in any case, given the large quantities of fat and gristle). From January 1942 meat and canned tuna were replaced by 'minestrone', a vegetable soup supplemented in theory by 100g more of pasta, 10g of dried vegetables and 60g of cheese, which could be substituted by canned fish twice a week. Locally purchased food was scarce and expensive, and mutton proved unsatisfactory since it could not be braised in its own juices (which was the custom in the army, using the broth to cook pasta and rice), for the simple reason that it absorbed olive oil, and nothing was left to flavour either pasta or minestrone. As a result combat troops, whenever on the move, were often supplied with just 400g of army biscuits and one can of tinned meat. Unsurprisingly troops in Cyrenaica suffered from scarcity of food supplies until the summer of 1941, when they were joined by field kitchens and bakeries, and rest camps were established. However, this problem could not be easily solved in 1942, when the front at El Alamein overstretched the supply lines. The gulf between officers and other ranks exacerbated complaints about food; although mostly in the rear, officers had their own mess where they could eat pasta along with tinned meat or fish at the cost of five lire, plus two for water.

Water supply was another major problem, sometimes solved by desalinization. This, however, produced water that Italian soldiers did not like. Rations were often limited to one litre per day, sometimes less, as in September 1942 at El Alamein, when the daily ration was cut to half a litre. Inadequate food and water, along with environmental conditions, brought

'TRENTO' DIVISION STRONGPOINT, EL ALAMEIN 1942

The defence line built by Axis troops at El Alamein was the strongest and the most important of the Western Desert war. Protected by large and dense minefields and barbed wire, the German and Italian strongpoints faced unavoidable onslaught by the Eighth Army under unfavourable circumstances. Because of the nature of the terrain it was not possible to build protected shelters with roofs to give cover from artillery shells and splinters, and the desert sand often made the digging of foxholes impossible. The alternative was, as in this case, a mixed strongpoint, which was often favoured by the Italian infantry and which accommodated riflemen as well as machine-gun nests and one gun position (either a 20mm Breda anti-aircraft gun or a 47mm anti-tank gun). This particular strongpoint, built at El Alamein, included three machine-gun nests and one position for a 47/32 anti-tank gun deployed along a 20-odd metre stretch, with the machine-gun nests at intervals of about 6m from each other. Riflemen taking cover in the communicating trenches rather than the machine-gun nests or gun position also added extra firepower. At El Alamein Italian soldiers wore a variety of uniforms, including the European grey-green uniform, out of necessity given the scarcity of tropical uniforms but also because the climate that, especially at night, often required protection from cold and the use of an overcoat. The weapons shown here include, apart from the 6.5mm Carcano rifle, the 8mm heavy machine gun Breda 37 which, along with the Fiat 35 (the same calibre), was the most widely distributed heavy machine gun of the Italian army, also favoured by British and Commonwealth troops. With a rate of fire of 550–600 rounds per minute, the machine gun was hampered by being fed with ammunition clips (28 rounds per clip), although a skilled crew could fire long bursts by inserting one clip straight after another. The 47/32mm gun was the standard Italian anti-tank gun during the war; able to penetrate up to 37mm-thick armour at 700m, but from 1941–42 it was used only to immobilize enemy tanks by firing at their tracks. Conceived for pack transport, it weighed only 78kg and could be dismantled; it was usually sited in a dugout with a circular trench all round, which enabled the crew to shift its position as needed.

A 20mm Breda 30 gun position in the desert, apparently not looking for enemy aircraft. The use of civilian items of clothing, such as the waistcoat worn by the second man from the left, was not unusual although this practice was more typical of other fronts such as Yugoslavia or Russia. (Ernesto G. Vitetti)

widespread dysentery; since it was simply not possible to treat all those affected in the field hospitals, many had to live with the disease, sometimes for long periods. It is probably thanks to the army's emphasis on physical fitness that Italian soldiers in North Africa did not suffer greatly from their overextended periods in the theatre and from poor diet. The available figures for soldiers hospitalized in Egypt in September 1942 are in fact low (269 officers, 319 NCOs, and 3,981 other ranks), especially when compared with widespread sickness amongst the newly arrived German troops, which suggests either the Italian soldiers were better able to acclimatize, or that the army medical service did not allow hospitalization.

The medical service in North Africa suffered from lack of motor transport as well; field hospitals were deep in the rear, leaving only the divisional medical sections close to the front. Lacking both personnel (medical staff in particular) and equipment, these could deal only with light wounds, all others having to be sent back to field hospitals whenever possible. Because of the lack of ambulances, it was not unusual for soldiers to die while waiting for transport or during the journey; in 1942 many of the wounded from the 'Folgore' division who needed treatment would die because the nearest field hospital was 12 hours' march away. On the other hand the wounded of the 'Ariete' division, which had a relatively large number of captured vehicles, could be swiftly recovered from the battlefield and brought back to the field hospitals. Logistics also caused many problems for medical supplies, and units at the front often lacked medication. The problem became quite serious in 1942, and it could be temporarily solved only thanks to the medication and supplies captured at Tobruk and at Mersa Matruh.

EXPERIENCE OF BATTLE

From the point of view of the historian, Italian soldiers in North Africa seem to have disappeared from the scene after defeat in the winter of 1940–41; all accounts feature Rommel and the Afrika Korps. However, the fact is that the Italians were always on the battlefield, even after their disastrous defeat, but then, as now, they were viewed with contempt. This sometimes proved to be a fatal mistake.

Before the start of Operation *Crusader* in November 1941 the men of the 4th County of London Yeomanry ('CLY') were reassuringly told how inefficient the Italian soldiers and their tanks were; on 19 November, the day after the start of *Crusader*, the 22nd Armoured Brigade of 7th Armoured Division attacked the Italian positions at Bir El Gubi, held by the 'Ariete' division. The 2nd Royal Gloucestershire Hussars ('RGH') overran the positions of the heavy weapons battalion of the 8° Reggimento Bersaglieri, still deploying and with their guns aboard lorries. Taken by surprise, many Italian soldiers gave themselves up, only to be ignored by the British tank crews, which continued to advance north of Bir El Gubi. Before long the 'Ariete' tank regiment counterattacked and the 2nd RGH was under fire from concealed anti-tank positions. After two and a half hours of combat the regiment withdrew, only to be fired upon by the same Bersaglieri unit that they had earlier overrun, which, in the meantime, had deployed its guns. At dusk the 2nd RGH had lost 30 of its 46 tanks while the 3rd CLY, which had wisely taken custody of the Italian POWs at the time of their surrender, had lost only four (the 4th CLY, initially held in reserve, lost eight).

Italian losses were also high, including 34 tanks, 25 killed and 177 wounded or missing, and eventually 22nd Armoured Brigade could recover some of the tanks lost from the battleground. The clash at Bir El Gubi on 19 November 1941 was somehow to mark a new start for the Italian soldiers in North Africa, while the men of 22nd Armoured Brigade no longer had illusions that fighting

Portrait of the crew of an M13 tank of the 'Ariete' division in the desert, the man on the right being a *sottotenente* who has applied metal rank badges to his overalls. Interestingly, all are wearing different types of overalls, although all are armed with the 9mm Beretta 34 pistol in a holster and all wear the much-needed leather helmet. (Ernesto G. Vitetti)

the Italians was no cakewalk. As Tenente Roberto Rosselli of the VIII Battaglione Corazzato, 'Ariete's' 132° Reggimento Corazzato remembered, his driver made a simple remark when advancing against enemy tanks: 'the time has come, we've been waiting for this for a long time'. Although wounded, at the end of the day, Tenente Rosselli and his crew had not only gained precious experience, but also the belief that they could fight back.

A heavy 81mm mortar manned by *Bersaglieri*, ready to fire from its dugout position. Interestingly, these soldiers wear a real assortment of uniforms: a *sahariana*, a grey-green jacket, and an early-style *camiciotto sahariano*, although all (apart from the officer) wear tropical pith helmets. (Ernesto G. Vitetti)

However, it still seems difficult for historians to acknowledge one very simple fact: Italian soldiers could and would fight, in spite of their many shortcomings. It is not unusual to find in the accounts of the second Alamein battle comments about two battalions of the 62° Reggimento of the 'Trento' division that, facing the 9th Australian Division, at the start of Operation *Lightfoot* on the night of 23 October 1942, fell under Eighth Army's artillery fire and fled the battle scene, leaving a gap in the line. This is how Rommel told the story in his account of the battle, but one has only to check the available German records and the official Australian history to discover a different story; those Italian soldiers did not flee the battle scene, but were hit heavily by an artillery barrage that killed more than half of them. Before the rest had time to reorganize, the

G | **FIELD HOSPITAL IN THE DESERT, 1942**

The field organization of the Italian medical service was not particularly effective, at least for front-line soldiers. Divisions had only a medical section at their disposal, while medical companies were attached to corps commands, and field hospitals, themselves attached as needed either to a corps or to an army, were usually located far from the front in areas untouched by enemy fire. As a result severely wounded soldiers needed to be transported to the field hospital, which might take some time (it was not unusual to be evacuated to a field hospital in a matter of hours) with all the risks associated with a delay in treatment. Divisional medical sections, made up of transport and stretcher-bearer detachments, were entrusted with the task of recovering the wounded from the battlefield and moving them to first aid posts, one of which being (generally speaking) formed within each battalion of the division. There the lightly wounded would be treated on the spot, soon to be returned to their unit, while those requiring further treatment had to be transferred by the section, which had its own ambulances, to the nearest field hospital. Italian field hospitals were not usually large, with an average of 50 beds, although the number could be doubled if necessary. As a general rule field hospitals were stationary, although they did follow the troops whenever deep advances or withdrawals took place, as was the case with the Axis advance to El Alamein in June to July 1942. Field hospitals worked closely with the corps medical companies, which could be deployed close to the front line when needed; this required the allocation of motor transport from the corps or the army as field hospitals did not have their own. Here we see a field hospital being set up in Egypt, with a medical captain wearing a standard tropical field uniform with two stretcher-bearers (in Italian *portaferiti*), dressed in a mixture of uniforms that include the grey-green European jacket. Although wearing Red Cross armbands, both are armed with 1889 Bodeo revolvers (as revealed by the pistol holsters); one carries a special, larger canteen with a cup underneath and the other a first aid kit, mostly consisting of bandages. It is worth noting that each soldier had his own small first aid kit, to be carried in the inside pocket of his jacket. Both stretcher-bearers carry a gas mask in their bag, the Italian army always being concerned about possible chemical warfare attacks.

Laying telephone wires to ensure field communication, a group of Italian engineers (probably in Egypt) show a very relaxed attitude toward their uniforms, wearing mostly shorts and woollen socks. Most of these field communication lines would be easily interrupted by enemy artillery. (Filippo Cappellano)

The effect of windstorms on a field tent camp, that on the right (made from camouflage tent quarters) being almost buried under the sand. The Ghibli was one of the most annoying features of the climate, lasting for several days and causing temperatures to rise. (Filippo Cappellano)

advancing Australian infantry stormed their positions taking them prisoners. Not all of them, though; one company of the II Battaglione of 62° Reggimento continued to fight, like the artillery. As recalled by Sergente Poletto of the divisional communications company, on the evening of 23 October a real torrent of fire fell on the positions held by the men of the 'Trento', hitting one strongpoint after another. All the veterans of the division recalled this experience as something never seen before, an apparently endless hail of fire. Yet, Poletto and his comrades fell asleep waiting for sunrise, which brought with it the unpleasant surprise of the approaching enemy. Ordered to withdraw to the divisional HQ, Poletto and his men found the remnants of 62° Reggimento there, soon joined by the armour of the 'Littorio' division. As he recalled, having failed to press on harder, the enemy had lost a chance to break through the Italian positions.

To the south, in the 51st Highland Division sector, the British 2nd Armoured Brigade broke through the German positions attacking those of 'Trento's' 46° Reggimento di Artiglieria, which replied by firing at close range against the British tanks. A counterattack by the tanks and self-propelled guns of 'Littorio' armoured division eventually prevented a breakthrough in the area. The following day, it was the turn of the British 9th Armoured Brigade, which overran one company of 'Trento's' 61° Reggimento, only to fall prey again to the guns of 46° Reggimento, eventually halting its advance west of the Myteirya ridge. As night fell, the 'Trento' division's strength was down to two infantry and two artillery battalions. Soldato Vittorio Valicella of 6th Battery of III Battaglione, 46° Reggimento di Artiglieria, recalled, as did others, the violent intensity of the artillery barrage ('like an earthquake') on the night of 23 October, but also the pride in receiving news about the divisional artillery that fought back the advancing British tanks, and how the final strongholds of the division fought to the last. During the morning of 27 October he witnessed three lorries bringing Italian wounded back to the field hospital near El Daba, 15km away, and he considered how dangerous their journey would have been. Displaying no red cross, those lorries could

Generale d'Armata Ettore Bastico, centre, with some of his officers. He was Commander-in-Chief in North Africa from 27 July 1941 to 16 August 1942, when his command was redesignated Comando Superiore della Libia (Libya High Command). Although Rommel was in theory subordinated to him, there was never a direct chain of command. (Filippo Cappellano)

be strafed by enemy fighters at any time. Even in the rear water was scarce and food limited to army biscuits and tinned meat, since all motor transport was being used to bring forward much-needed ammunition. For 11 days Valicella and his comrades stood with their battery which, on 3 November, was down to a few men; the following day news of the order to withdraw reached them; they jumped on their vehicles driving west, eventually rejoining the remnants of the only Italian division that withdrew from El Alamein – the 'Trieste' – at El Gazala, on 13 November.

The 'Trento' division's baptism of fire was in April 1941, during Rommel's first drive into Cyrenaica and the unsuccessful attacks against the Tobruk fortress, which also brought about 'Brescia' division's baptism of fire. On the night of 30 April 1941 a mixed unit of the division took part in the attack against the Tobruk fortress, starting the Ras el Mdauuar battle; advancing at night the Italian soldiers passed through the gaps in the wires but, like their German counterparts, mistook their position and drifted to the right. Nevertheless, they managed to seize one strongpoint and attacked another just north of the area where the 15. Panzer-Division attacked, but the British tank counterattack halted their attack at first, then with Australian infantry support the men of the 20° Reggimento di Fanteria were pushed back. Their losses totalled 400. Nevertheless, the division was deployed on the western side of the Tobruk fortress along with two German battalions. This was the first combat experience of the division that, 18 months later, would be annihilated at El Alamein; a report by one of the officers of the division, written after the 1942 battle, accurately summarizes the experience of war in North Africa for Italian soldiers. Infantry regiments were under strength, in spite of new reinforcements that turned out to lack both the necessary training and the willingness to fight. Soldiers were tired; many had spent more than a year in North Africa, the division had been on the line almost constantly since May and overall conditions were far from ideal. Lack of water caused poor hygiene, and sickness was also brought about by a lack of medication and inadequate food rations (there were no fruit or vegetables,

Truck-borne infantry. It is interesting that they are wearing the 1940-model greenish-khaki tropical uniform and pith helmets but no neck sling to support ammunition pouches. The fact that they are wearing brand new uniforms without lapel badges (apart from the national star) suggests these are either replacements or soldiers back from a rest camp. (Filippo Cappellano)

only scant fresh meat, and bread was often mouldy). Motor transport was scarce and the officers, mostly substantive, lacked technical skill. With units broken down into different strongpoints, and having no reserves, there was nothing the commanders could do when the time came to fight.

The 'Bologna' division, after deployment on the Djebel, took position around Tobruk in late August, replacing the 'Trento' to the east. On 21 November 1941 the Tobruk garrison, British 70th Division and 32nd Army Tank Brigade, attacked the positions held by the 'Bologna' and the German 90. leichte Afrika Division attempting to break through the besieging forces. Italian soldiers were pushed back, and three of their strongpoints seized; Tenente Alessio Lucchini, commanding a 20mm gun battery of the 205° Reggimento di Artiglieria, withdrew with his men who pulled the guns themselves, establishing a new strongpoint along with a mixed infantry unit. For four days it held out against enemy attacks, but a more forceful attack on the 25th saw the strongpoint collapse. Lucchini, along with those who managed to withdraw, made his way back to the regimental HQ while the Tobruk garrison established contact with the advancing units of Eighth Army. Lucchini kept waiting for reinforcements to counterattack, but these never

H **TUNISIAN FRONT, 1942–43**

Following the Allied landings in Morocco and Algeria and the Axis building of the Tunisian bridgehead, soon to be followed by the evacuation of the last Axis troops from Libya, the war in North Africa entered its final stage in quite a different environment. The troops no longer had to deal with the heath and the sands of the desert but with a more 'Mediterranean' climate that also required different uniforms. Although the grey-green European uniforms had already been in use in both 1940 and 1942, mostly because of a shortage of tropical uniforms, they more or less became the rule in Tunisia. The cavalryman, temporarily assigned to traffic control (2), wears the standard grey-green uniform with a helmet that has been painted grey-green, typical cavalry leggings and cross belt used both by mounted and motorized personnel. For his duties he has been provided with a white armband and white gloves, along with the standard signalling disk. The black cross stencilled on his helmet was the badge used by the men of the 'Nizza', 'Piemonte', 'Savoia', and 'Genova' cavalry regiments, the former having its III Gruppo Corazzato in North Africa along with the 'Ariete' division. In other cases standard uniform items normally in use in Europe were worn together with tropical uniforms; this *Bersagliere* of the 5° Reggimento Bersaglieri (1) wears a waterproof cotton windcheater over his tropical uniform, complete with a tropical pith helmet decorated with cockerel feathers which, following quite common practice since 1942, has had its national cockade and metal badge replaced by the same stencilled badge that is normally found on steel helmets. This is one of the two standard models of windcheater, the other (pullover style) being fastened at the front with laces. On his belt this *Bersagliere* carries the canvas and leather ammunition pouches (worn in pairs) normally issued to cyclist or motorcyclist *Bersaglieri* units, while in his hand he holds a captured Boys 0.55 Mk I anti-tank rifle. The airlanding infantry division 'La Spezia', scheduled to take part in the invasion of Malta, was sent to Libya in November 1942 and subsequently redeployed in Tunisia in January 1943. This sergeant of the 80° Reggimento di Artiglieria (3) (note the lapel badges) wears standard tropical uniform (with woollen socks replacing the puttees), including the model 1942 field cap, with tropical overcoat, made of greenish-khaki wool, a widely used item whenever available. He is armed with a model 91, 6.5mm Carcano rifle for special troops, with foldable bayonet fixed to the gun muzzle.

A Breda 30 light machine-gun team showing, on the left, the large wooden box used to carry two spare barrels and, inside, other spare parts. The ammunition box would be carried by the soldier on the right who, like his comrade, is firing a 6.5mm 91 Carcano rifle with foldable bayonet. (Ernesto G. Vitetti)

came and, on the morning of 26 November 1941, his position was surrounded by the tanks of the 32nd Tank Brigade, and he was taken prisoner.

If the experience of battle at the front was hard, life in the rear was not easy either; soldiers serving at Tripoli may have been regarded by those at the front as war dodgers, but the many air attacks against the harbour and the city and the heavy bombardments all too often made it seem like a front-line position. There was also the 'other' war in the desert, in the Fezzan where the Italian and Libyan soldiers fought against Long Range Desert Group, also raiding Cyrenaica (itself defended by the Italians), and the Free French forces from Chad. Bringing supplies from Tripoli to the front was no easy job either, as the driver Pietro Zunino was to discover soon after his arrival at Tripoli and his first journey with a fully laden SPA 38 lorry; travelling during the night he was surprised to meet other vehicles travelling back with their lights off, something which amused him. He was lucky to meet two stationary cars and a group of people, who waved their arms and shouted at him to switch off his lights. Zunino halted the lorry and before he could ask why there was all the fuss, his lorry was showered with machine-gun fire and an aircraft roared overhead. He jumped out seeking cover, while everyone else disappeared. Still stunned, he got back to his lorry and started to drive again, this time with the lights turned off. That was his baptism of fire by the RAF.

In spite of the clichés and unfavourable conditions, the Italian soldiers in North Africa fought their war, to say the least, sometimes even performing well, and in some cases right to the end. On 19 April 1943 the New Zealand Division attacked the Enfidaville Line, its 5th Brigade hitting a small ridge named Takrouna, defended by a battalion of 'Trieste's' 66° Reggimento, more a mixture of stragglers from different units. For two days the Italians and the New Zealanders fiercely struggled for control of the small village on top of the ridge, with both sides attacking and counterattacking similar to the fighting in Stalingrad or Cassino. Eventually the New Zealanders succeeded in taking control of Takrouna, although their advance was in fact halted; 5th Brigade losses in this particular struggle numbered 459. At Takrouna 318 Italian and five German prisoners were taken, the bulk of the 568 Italian and 164 German prisoners taken by the brigade at the end of the battle. Less than a month later, the Axis forces in North Africa surrendered.

BELIEF AND BELONGING

One of the reasons behind the many clichés and platitudes often repeated about Italian soldiers in North Africa is the lack of any clear image of Italian troops after their defeat in the winter of 1940–41. On the one hand we have the German Afrika Korps, with its legendary commander Erwin Rommel, and on the other the British (and Commonwealth and Imperial) Eighth Army, the famous 'Desert Rats' (a name borrowed from the 7th Armoured Division, in fact), and the equally legendary commander Bernard Law Montgomery. The Italians, however, seem to disappear in a kind of haze, unknown and unseen by the many, partly because they did not have a legendary name, or famous commander. This fact certainly affected the image of the Italian soldier in North Africa in post-war accounts, but it is also necessary to consider how it affected the morale of the Italian troops, as well as their sense of belief and belonging. After the Italian surrender in 1943, Generalfeld Marschall Kesselring realized that inadequate war propaganda was one of the reasons for disaffection in what was eventually seen as 'Mussolini's war'. In fact Italian propaganda was rather blunt-edged, focusing before and during the war on Britain and how she opposed Italy, preventing her from achieving her

A mixed Italian-German traffic roadblock in Tunisia, with two cavalrymen from the Nizza Cavalleria regiment to the right. In 1942 the III Gruppo Nizza was the reconnaissance unit of the 'Ariete' division, fighting as an independent unit in Tunisia in 1943. (Filippo Cappellano)

Italian soldiers jubilant after entering Bardia in June 1942, immediately before the advance into Egypt. The Marmon Herrington armoured car seems to have been pressed into Italian service. (Filippo Cappellano)

goals. It is questionable how effective this was for the individual soldier, however; it is not customary in Italian culture to explain fully the reasons behind a course of action, and even Fascist propaganda never went so far as to provide the troops with a real reason why they were fighting. Troops were also greatly affected by a lack of belonging resulting from a failure to link them to their unit, commanders or even to the theatre of operation.

Following the destruction of Tenth Army in February 1941, there was not an Italian army fighting in North Africa again, at least not until the Panzer Armee Afrika was reorganized as First Italian Army in Tunisia in February 1943. The Italian army corps fighting under Rommel's command was in fact led by a number of different Italian generals, the same as the divisions under their command, and yet no leading personality ever emerged (at least not one that stood out). This whole time, Rommel, although appreciated, was never really regarded by the Italian troops as their leader. Frequent rotation of unit commanders, particularly facing the absence of an army commander, certainly prevented soldiers from identifying themselves with an individual commander or even unit. The CAM, later XX Corpo, had six commanders during the North African campaign, XXI Corpo had only two, but X Corpo had three, even though it was operational only from January to November 1942. Divisional commanders frequently changed in a similar way; 'Trento' division had seven commanders, 'Pavia' and 'Brescia' six commanders each, 'Ariete' four, 'Bologna' and 'Trieste' three each, and 'Savona' (disbanded January 1942) two. The few notable commanders, those who might have risen to stand above others and even Rommel, did not last long enough or arrived at the scene too late; these include CAM corps commander Generale d'Armata Gastone Gambara (sacked by Rommel in December 1941, who was eventually picked by him in late 1943 as the chief of staff of the new Italian army in German-controlled Italy), and Generale d'Armata, later Maresciallo d'Italia, Giovanni Messe who took command of First Army. Messe (who rose from the ranks) was a well-known and respected commander who earned his fame on the Eastern Front, and, certainly in the opinion of Italian soldiers, might have risen to the same level as Rommel and Montgomery. But he arrived on the scene only when the war in North Africa was practically lost, leaving no clear account of himself (it is worth noting that after the Italian surrender he became chief of general staff in Allied-controlled Italy).

Success on the battlefield would provide a sense of belonging mainly to those few elite units such as the 'Ariete' and the 'Trieste' divisions, shaped by their performances during *Crusader*, or to an all-volunteer unit such as the Giovani Fascisti regiment, which experienced success in the Bir El Gubi battle of 19 December 1941 helping to create a real sense of belonging. However, most of the other units just faded away in a rather heterogeneous blend of infantry 'cannon fodder', their soldiers being not only victims of the non-elite status of those units, but also of the classic image of the war in the Western Desert as a mechanized war. Unsurprisingly, these soldiers developed a widespread, ever-growing, resentment against the war dodgers in the rearguard, also feeling that they had been assigned a kind of backstage role in a war that had its real 'stars' in the armour and the mechanized units.

The fact that the Italian army in North Africa was composed of different realities did also play a role in the failure to develop a proper sense of belief and belonging that

A field workshop for engines and other mechanical repairs, with the mechanics wearing standard blue overalls and grey-green side caps with no insignia. Only a few of these mobile workshops were available, in spite of the dire need to recover and repair vehicles from the battlefield. (Filippo Cappellano)

afflicted a large proportion of Italian soldiers; it is true that in every army those who are at the front always blame those in the rear for being war dodgers, but in this case resentment seemed to be fully justified. Lack of rotation from front to rear, either at the level of single units or of individual soldiers, further exacerbated the idea that those who were serving in the rearguard such as in Tripolitania successfully managed to avoid the dangers and discomforts of the battle front, and were blamed for every discomfort and disadvantage suffered by the fighting soldiers – the faulty postal service and the lack of food and water, just to mention two. The huge gulf that all

A 149/12 field gun firing early in the war, probably 1940, as suggested by the gun crew still wearing a pre-war grey-green uniform with coloured fabric at the neck, and by the very neat appearance of their pith helmets. (Filippo Cappellano)

Line-up of Italian volunteers recruited in Tunisia in the Kasbah barracks in Tunis. These recruits are all wearing grey-green field uniform along with equipment, but have not been supplied with any kind of badge or insignia, not even the lapel stars of the Italian soldiers. (Ernesto G. Vitetti)

too often divided officers from the other ranks also contributed to a failure in developing a real sense of belief and belonging amongst the Italian soldiers; seeing the example of Rommel, a general who openly experienced the same dangers and discomforts as his own soldiers, the average Italian soldier found it hard to understand why, in the Italian army, discomforts affected only them, and not their officers.

It is not surprising, taking these factors into account, that soldiers from some of the elite units such as the 'Ariete' armoured, the 'Trieste' motorized, and the 'Folgore' parachute divisions were able to develop not only a stronger sense of *esprit de corps* and of camaraderie, but also a deeper sense of belief and belonging than most of the other soldiers belonging to the infantry units ever did. And yet, the fact that these soldiers kept fighting for months and years on end, also performing well, and even beyond the call of duty, does reveal the truth behind the one comment made about the average Italian soldier: that in spite of all the weakness of its army, from the lack of adequate weapons to the lack of training, the poor command and leadership, and an overall shortage of equipment and supplies, the Italian soldier would nevertheless keep fighting, all too often in conditions that soldiers belonging to other armies would have considered unacceptable.

Such a widespread sense of inferiority, in terms of weapons, command, and equipment, down to actual success (or lack of) on the battlefield, did eventually contribute to the shaping of the one, real sense of belief and belonging that would actually unite all the Italian soldiers in North Africa – the idea that even in spite of, or because of, all the weaknesses and failures of their army, whatever they achieved was in fact the result of their own courage and valour more than the result of material or technical superiority over the enemy. And it was this sense of individual courage and valour (as opposed to the idea of a nation and an army that might even betray their own citizens and soldiers), which was the one factor that contributed to the moulding of a strong sense of national pride against the enemy – an enemy all too often seen not as described by the propaganda, but rather as an adversary of valour, and one whose victories could be almost entirely attributed to material and technical superiority.

All this helps to explain why, in the post-war years, the Italians focused their attention almost entirely on one single battle: El Alamein. Clearly the Italian soldiers, and their units, were not at their best in the offensive, particularly in a highly mobile, mechanized warfare. They were, on the contrary, well suited to fighting a defensive war, in which they actually excelled, particularly when it was fought on much more familiar terrain such as Tunisia. This explains why the Italians did not focus on the battles fought in Cyrenaica, around Tobruk, largely dominated by the German Afrika Korps. Tunisia always represented a kind of 'last stand' battle, certainly lacking the epic dimensions and greatness of a decisive battle, such as El Alamein. This would not only see the majority of Italian soldiers all fighting together, but it also shows how deeply rooted the sense of sacrifice and of individual valour are in the Italian soldier. This is because the fighting at El Alamein, focusing almost entirely on the second battle, is seen as a kind of doomed battle, that the Italian soldiers fought, well aware of their inferiority in terms of *matériel* (for which Mussolini is always blamed), and yet still proved their courage and valour. Still, even in the present day, these feelings are not embraced by the majority of people or the army; El Alamein, the name that for the present-day Italian represents the North African campaign as a whole, is mostly associated with units such as the 'Folgore' paratroopers and the 'Ariete' armoured, only part of the Italian army, rather than with the army as a whole. A clear sign of fading memory and of lack of understanding.

A provisional rest area for Italian soldiers moving to and from the front (the board reads *alloggio per i militari in transito*, quarters for soldiers in transit). The soldier standing on the left, wearing shorts and a shirt, is a Bersagliere with a typical red fez with blue tassel. (Filippo Cappellano)

AFTER THE BATTLE

Of the tens of thousands of Italian soldiers who fought in North Africa between June 1940 and May 1943 only a few thousand, mostly wounded and sick who could not be adequately treated in Libya, were able to avoid death or capture, having been sent back home before the final surrender. For almost all the Italian soldiers posted to a unit in North Africa, either actively fighting or in the rearguard, such an assignment was going to be a one-way ticket because of the near impossibility of rotating men and units to and from Italy. For those who could not make it back home, the only possible chance if one succeeded in not being killed (and that could happen in many different ways), was quite simple: to sooner or later become a prisoner of war in the hands of the enemy. And such an ending to a soldier's war differed quite considerably according to which army had taken him prisoner.

Until late 1942 only the British and Commonwealth forces took Italian soldiers prisoner, all in all about 350,000. Although personal accounts differ on the subject, one can say that on the whole treatment was generally fair even if it was harsh in some cases. After an initial period in camps in Egypt or Palestine, Italian POWs were sent to other camps in other African states such as South Africa, or overseas, to India and even Australia. After 1942–43 Italian POWs were mostly kept in POW camps in North Africa, and some of them were sent to Great Britain. In 1942–43 another large batch of Italian soldiers were taken prisoner by US forces in Tunisia, some 50,000 of them being sent to the United States and another 100,000 being kept in POW camps in Algeria and Morocco. A few thousand Italian soldiers became French POWs, either captured directly or handed over by the British and the Americans.

The living conditions of Italian POWs differed according to various factors: the army that captured them, the location of POW camps, and their rank. Many of the rank and file found that working in the fields of an

A Solothurn anti-tank rifle manned by men of the IV Battaglione Contro Carro Granatieri di Sardegna (anti-tank battalion from the Sardinian grenadiers), attached to the 'Trento' division in 1942. Note the painted badge on the pith helmet. (Filippo Cappellano)

A soldier, very likely a driver, eats his rations standing on top of the bonnet of his lorry. Although he wears both a pith helmet and grey-green trousers with puttees and boots, he is bare chested. (Filippo Cappellano)

Australian, South African or British farm, presented similar living conditions to those of their original background and were not at all unpleasant, much better in fact than remaining idle in a POW camp. Not surprisingly, being also used to emigration, some would start a new life after the war in one of these foreign countries, such as South Africa. Others remember their time as a POW with differing degrees of unpleasantness; hunger and sickness were widespread, the guards reckless, and there was the constant worry of being far away from their families.

Changes came following the Italian surrender on 8 September 1943; the splitting in two of the country – the Germans and their Fascist allies in the north, the Allies in the south – also affected the Italian POWs. Offered the choice of volunteering to support the Allied war effort, most agreed to do so, even though all too often it brought no real improvement to their conditions, apart from increased use as labour. Some Italian POWs refused to cooperate with the Allies – not always for political reasons, in some cases more a simple matter of pride. In this case the treatment reserved for them would change; to avoid clashes with the other POWs they were moved to other, specially selected, POW camps and encountered harsher treatment. Some 6,000 Italian POWs in American hands refused to cooperate and, in doing so, had their food rations reduced (in some cases down to starvation levels) and experienced strict discipline and punishment. Of the different cases recorded, the officers' POW camp at Hereford, Texas, became particularly infamous given the really harsh treatment reserved for those Italian POWs that did not cooperate.

On the other hand, those that cooperated in the camps in the United States enjoyed treatment that sometimes offered better conditions than those they had faced during the North African campaign; there was plenty of food, their work was not hard, camps and clothes were clean. These POWs formed 'Italian Service Units' employed to support American rail transport, for repair work, for work in agriculture and wherever needed. Much to the annoyance of the French authorities, the same kind of treatment was reserved for Italian POWs in camps in North Africa; some of these would make their way back to Italy after the Allied advance into the peninsula, while a further 40,000 were even taken to southern France after the Allied landings in Provence in August 1944, eventually to advance along with Seventh US Army to Germany.

The worst treatment reserved for the Italian POWs was by the French, resentful of Italian aggression in June 1940, the 'stab in the back'. The Allied forces handed some 40,000 Italian POWs over to the French after the end of the North African campaign, in violation of international agreements, which required prisoners of war to be held in custody by the nations that captured them. These Italian soldiers were the subject of harsh treatment both at the hands of the French civilians, mostly while being transferred, and at the hands of the French military, particularly by the colonial troops who treated the Italians in the POW camps with a certain degree of cruelty. French officers hardly intervened, and only to suggest the Italians join the French Foreign Legion. It is not surprising that the death rate amongst the Italian POWs held in North Africa was six times greater in French camps than in American or British POW camps.

It must be said that, with such a huge number of POWs and, in spite of their being dispersed to the four corners of the world, some attempts to escape were made, although the actual figures are not high; on average there was one escape for every thousand POWs. Attempts followed the classic practices common to all POWs across the world: underground tunnels, taking advantage of work outside the camps, or even exploiting the lack of adequate surveillance by guards. Almost every time these attempts ended the same way; the prisoners were captured again, and they would spend four weeks in the 'cooler' back in their camps. Some succeeded; a group of Italian POWs escaped and reached Turkey from Palestine, while others escaped from their camps in India to reach the Portuguese enclave of Goa. Others escaped from their POW camps in Africa, eventually making their way to Mozambique. Not one of them was able to make the road back home, at least before the war ended. Only two officers succeeded in reaching Italy in 1945 after the end of the war, having escaped from their POW camp in Egypt; both were still being hunted.

Some lucky prisoners were able to escape from camps in Algeria, finding no other way to avoid being caught than hiding in the kasbah of Algiers, exploiting the fact that it was 'out of bounds' for Allied troops. Others were able to escape from the French POW camps in Morocco, but in this case they escaped only as far as the American camps and were held there, thanks to the complicity of the Italian-American guards. The strangest escape was of three Italian officers who made their way out of a British POW camp in Kenya, only to climb the 15,000ft Mount Kenya in order to plant the Italian flag on top. Once back, they handed themselves over to their guards.

For many Italian soldiers, time spent in POW camps pushed the experience of fighting in the North African campaign into the background, particularly for those who had been captured in 1940–41. After the end of the war and

An R2 portable, tactical radio set being used by an artillery lieutenant, almost certainly to report targets to the artillery batteries of his unit. Spotting for the artillery was difficult in the desert, and it is recalled that an officer devised a truck-mounted ladder for this purpose. (Filippo Cappellano)

A captured Bren carrier pressed into Italian service, the only changes apparently being the addition of an 8mm Breda 37 heavy machine gun and, on the side, the Latin motto *Memento Audere Semper*, made famous by the poet D'Annunzio. (Filippo Cappellano)

their release, the memory of the campaign started to emerge, particularly for those taken prisoner in 1942–43. The memory of hard times and fiercely fought battles did not produce, however, any collective memory. The long period of time spent in the theatre by most of the soldiers helped to form bonds, often intense and long-lasting amongst the surviving veterans, but these were almost exclusively formed within the boundaries of whichever unit those men belonged to. The veterans of the Giovani Fascisti regiment formed a veterans' association based, with its museum, in the house of their former unit commander, while up to the present day the veterans of the 'Folgore' division represent the real backbone of the lasting memory of both the El Alamein battle and of the unit itself.

But the most important contribution to the collective memory of the Italian soldiers in North Africa came in the 1960s with the building of the El Alamein memorial, achieved mostly thanks to the efforts and the sense of duty of Maggiore Paolo Caccia Dominioni, former commander of the XXXI Battaglione Guastatori. Between 1949 and 1959 he, along with a former NCO from his unit and some local guides, travelled some 360,000km in the Egyptian desert (sometimes across minefields) to search and recover the bodies of fallen Italian and non-Italian soldiers, the former gathered together in the memorial of point 33 which Caccia Dominioni, an architect by profession, built himself. Here, beneath a tower, are gathered the remains of 2,465 known Italian soldiers and a further 2,349 unknown, along with the Libyan soldiers that Caccia Dominioni deemed proper to remember.

BIBLIOGRAPHY AND FURTHER READING

Italian army records, manuals and reports from the archive of the Army Historical Branch, Rome.

Bedeschi, Giulio (editor), *Fronte d'Africa: c'ero anch'io* (Milan, 1979)

Bierman, John and Smith, Colin, *Alamein: War Without Hate* (London, 2003)

Bottaro, Alighiero, *Il vento del deserto. Africa settentrionale 1942–1945* (Milan, 2008)

Caccia Dominioni, Paolo (editor), *Le trecento ore a nord di Qattara. 23 ottobre – 6 novembre 1942* (Milan, 2012)

Cappellano, Filippo and Pignato, Nicola, *Andare contro i carri armati* (Udine, 2007)

Carrier, Richard, 'Assessing Fighting Power: The Case of the Italian Army in North Africa, June 1940 – May 1943'. Paper delivered at the Rome conference on the Desert War, 1940–1943; October 2012

Christie, Howard R., *Fallen Eagles: The Italian 10th Army in the Opening Campaign in the Western Desert, June 1940 – December 1940* (Fort Leavenworth, KS, 1999)

Ciampini, Danilo, 'La fanteria motorizzata tra modello ed esperienze: la Trieste in Africa settentrionale, 1941–42'. In: *Quaderno 1999 Società Italiana di Storia Militare*

Forty, George, *The Armies of Rommel* (London, 1997)

Gambella, Alfredo, *Ospite di Sua Maestà Britannica* (Gorizia, 2012)

Ilari, Virgilio, *Storia del servizio militare in Italia. Volume III: 'nazione militare' e 'fronte del lavoro' (1919–1943)* (Rome, 1990)

Loi, Salvatore, *'Aggredisci e vincerai'. Storia della divisione motorizzata Trieste* (Milan, 1983)

Messe, Giovanni, *La mia armata in Tunisia* (Milan, 2004)

Montanari, Mario, *Le operazioni in Africa Settentrionale*. Four volumes (Rome, 1985–1993)

Pignato, Nicola, *Armi della fanteria italiana nella seconda guerra mondiale* (Parma, 1978)

Pignato, Nicola, 'Prime esperienze italiane di guerra corazzata in Africa settentrionale'. In: *Quaderno 1999 Società Italiana di Storia Militare*

Rebora, Andrea, *Carri Ariete combattono* (Civitavecchia, 2009)

Serra, Enrico, *Carristi dell'Ariete* (Rome, 1979)

Trye, Rex, *Mussolini's Soldiers* (Shrewsbury, 1995)

Uccelli, Alfredo J., *Dai Balcani all'oceano di sabbia* (Milan, 2011)

Valicella, Vittorio, *Diario di guerra. Da El Alamein alla tragica ritirata 1942–1943* (Varese, 2009)

Viotti, Andrea, *Uniformi e distintivi dell'esercito italiano nella seconda guerra mondiale* (Rome, 1988)

Walker, Ian W., *Iron Hulls, Iron Hearts. Mussolini's Elite Armoured Divisions in North Africa* (Marlborough, Wilts., 2003)

Zapotoczny, Walter S., 'Italy's North African Misadventure. Was the Italian army simply a poor fighting force or was it doomed from the start by circumstance?' In: *World War II History*, January 2010

Zunino, Pietro, *Ricordi di guerra. Fronte dell'Africa Settentrionale e prigionia degli Inglesi 1940–'45* ('Savona', 2009)

INDEX

O - #0172 - 260220 - C16 - 248/184/4 - PB - 9781780968551